ROUTLEDGE LIBRARY EDITIONS:
EDUCATION

# CHANGING PATTERNS OF TEACHER EDUCATION

# CHANGING PATTERNS OF TEACHER EDUCATION

Edited by
MICHAEL RAGGETT &
MALCOLM CLARKSON

Volume 230

LONDON AND NEW YORK

First published in 1976

This edition first published in 2012
by Routledge
2 Park Square, Milton Park, Abingdon, Oxfordshire OX14 4RN

Simultaneously published in the USA and Canada
by Routledge
711 Third Avenue, New York, NY 10017

First issued in paperback 2014

*Routledge is an imprint of the Taylor and Francis Group, an informa company*

© 1976 Selection and editorial matter M St J Raggett and M W Clarkson

All rights reserved. No part of this book may be reprinted or reproduced or utilised in any form or by any electronic, mechanical, or other means, now known or hereafter invented, including photocopying and recording, or in any information storage or retrieval system, without permission in writing from the publishers.

*Trademark notice*: Product or corporate names may be trademarks or registered trademarks, and are used only for identification and explanation without intent to infringe.

*British Library Cataloguing in Publication Data*
A catalogue record for this book is available from the British Library

ISBN13: 978-0-415-50856-8 (Volume 230)
ISBN13: 978-0-415-75318-0 (pbk)

**Publisher's Note**
The publisher has gone to great lengths to ensure the quality of this reprint but points out that some imperfections in the original copies may be apparent.

**Disclaimer**
The publisher has made every effort to trace copyright holders and would welcome correspondence from those they have been unable to trace.

# CHANGING PATTERNS OF TEACHER EDUCATION

Edited by
Michael Raggett
& Malcolm Clarkson

The Falmer Press
in conjunction with
Ward Lock Educational

© Selection and editorial matter M St J Raggett and M W Clarkson 1976
All rights reserved. No part of this publication may be reproduced, stored in a retrieval system, or transmitted, in any form or by any means, electronic or mechanical, photocopying, recording or otherwise without the prior permission of the copyright owners.

ISBN 0 905273 00 1

First published 1976

Printed by the University of Sussex Printing Unit, Falmer, Sussex
for
The Falmer Press
116 Baker Street London W1M 2BB
Made in England

# Contents

| | |
|---|---|
| Foreword<br>M St J Raggett and M W Clarkson | 8 |
| Introduction<br>Norman Mackenzie | 10 |
| **The Changing Structures** | 23 |
| The re-organisation of the colleges of education: a critical overview<br>David Hencke | 25 |
| Aspects of institutional change<br>James Porter | 45 |
| Universities and colleges<br>Alec Ross | 56 |
| **The Changing Curriculum** | 69 |
| Principles and practice of validation<br>Edwin Kerr | 71 |
| Curriculum development in higher education<br>Anthony Becher | 91 |
| Modular course structures in higher education<br>Kenneth Gardner | 108 |
| **Discussion Papers** | 117 |
| The challenge of change<br>William Percival | 119 |
| Searching for a new identity<br>Norman Evans | 124 |
| Four major issues<br>Bernard Fisher | 131 |
| **Conclusions** | 140 |
| The Major issues: a summary of discussion reports<br>M St J Raggett and M W Clarkson | 142 |
| The future of teacher training<br>Roger Webster | 146 |
| New Patterns<br>M St J Raggett and M W Clarkson | 155 |
| The Contributors | 177 |

# Foreword

The Brighton Conference 1975 was devoted to an examination of the problems arising from the re-organisation of teacher education. By the Spring of 1975 it was clear that the demographic trends had dictated with inexorable logic that cuts in the number of teachers in training would be inevitable. Almost as inexorably, the type of pressure that had brought about the James Report and the White Paper on Education (Cmd 5174) had made it plain that the existing pattern of training and, indeed, of the whole of higher education could not continue. Circular 7/73 had followed pointing the way for the local development of higher education, the word development significantly becoming synonomous with re-organisation in many minds. Circular 6/74 had appeared to offer the colleges a salvation in new advanced courses, related to teacher education courses yet diversified in that they were not intended for students on teacher-training courses, but colleges had to run the gauntlet of new regional bodies and unfamiliar validating bodies. And if this wasn't enough, the situation had been capped by a falling demand for places in higher education and unprecedented national economic problems which made the rationalisation of resources necessary.

It appeared that changes of structures and emphases had taken place and were continuing to take place without debate, with scant consultation between those centrally involved and with little regard for preserving all that was best in teacher education. The significant thrust in curriculum development so often carried out under the twin pressures of haste and fear had resulted in the members of colleges becoming encapsulated in their institutions, too busy to digest the achievements of their colleagues in other colleges, too concerned with their own futures and too ill-informed to be able to discern the evolving pattern of development. It was in this situation that the Brighton Conference in April 1975 was organised to provide a framework for an academic consideration of the situation, its antecedents and its likely future developments.

The major objectives of the Conference were: first, to provide a forum for informed discussion of the recent decisions that had been made for re-organising the colleges; secondly, to consider the curricular changes that have followed re-organisation; and, thirdly, to look to the future and provide an opportunity to examine courses of action that might be most valuable if something worthwhile is to be salvaged. To meet these objectives, contributions were invited from those who had been centrally involved in the development of teacher education recently, such as members of the James Committee, a correspondent of the Times Higher Education Supplement, CNAA officers, principals of colleges and educational theorists and practitioners. The resulting papers were felt to be of significant interest and therefore it was decided that they should be published for the benefit of a wider audience.

The book has been divided into four sections. The first considers the structural changes resulting from mergers and changing institutional roles. The second section considers the changing curriculum; the third consists of discussion papers by three principals of colleges of education, and the fourth section summarises discussions and seeks to identify some future trends in teacher education. Roger Webster in his article suggests that radical curriculum change is usually precipitated only in response to crisis. That we now have a crisis there is no doubt; that curriculum change is occurring is apparent but if it will be radical still remains to be seen. The opportunity is present for a short time, it is to be hoped teacher educators will grasp it.

M St J Raggett<br>M W Clarkson

# Introduction

**Norman Mackenzie**

When one looks at what is happening in what were once colleges of education, one feels a bit like the man on the Titanic who had ordered a whisky and soda just as the ship hit the iceberg. 'I know I ordered ice,' he said, 'but this is simply ridiculous!.' One feels the same more or less about the iceberg known as Elizabeth House.

Obviously, in colleges like Brighton, one feels that impact very sharply. But we now have to face the new situation and not repine about lost possibilities. The best augury for the future in Sussex, I feel, is that we have been able to maintain good personal relationships with all those involved in the discussions about the fate of the College. Not only have we remained on speaking terms; we propose to work together more or less as we have in the past. I must, however, say in general terms that the separation between universities and colleges of education by the new policy is regrettable. In Sussex we have maintained a fairly widespread interest by academic faculty in education in general and teacher education in particular. It is bound to be less easy to keep such links in the new situation, or to persuade universities to allocate dwindling resources to pre-service and in-service education for teachers.

When I began to prepare my article, I let my mind go back to about 1970. Supposing, I thought, somebody had proposed the following. First, that it would be a good idea to create a new kind of college, a larger college, a college which is maybe a combination of several colleges, possibly a multi-campus college or a college which was formed by a merger with a polytechnic or even a university. Supposing, secondly, it was proposed to change the context and the professional prospects of the staff engaged in teacher education (in 1970 no one would have foreseen that about 1500 to 2000 of them would face either fairly rapid redundancy or substantial re-alignment of their professional prospects and a great many more would find themselves doing new, unfamiliar, and not necessarily congenial tasks in the period of re-adjustment). Supposing it had been argued that we ought rapidly to change the internal course structure to modular courses and to provide different combinations of subjects, new types of teaching groups, new modes of teaching, new kinds of awards. Supposing, fourthly, it had been argued that the role of universities in teacher education should be substantially reduced. Supposing it was planned greatly to enhance the powers of local education authorities and give them much more say in who or what happens in in-service education and in the education of teachers. Supposing we had learned, sixthly, that the DES planned to close a lot of colleges, abolish ATOs and set up new regional councils and to halve the numbers in teacher training by about 1980 - to say nothing about the familiar argument that we should abandon a monotechnic base for teacher education and fragment it in a different sort of way in different institutions. Finally, supposing we had been required, in addition to all this, to devise a greatly diversified academic structure. All that agenda would have seem impossibly large, complicated and highly controversial. Four year later it has been, in effect, that we shall do all these things - fast, without adequate discussion and without any additional resources.

That list makes me wonder what in fact is going to happen between now and 1981. Have we any kind of guidelines or perspective which could give us a reasonable framework for teacher education as these changes follow swiftly upon each other? David Hencke, in his article, writes about possible attempts to achieve a stability in the pattern. I must say I do not feel very much confidence in any statements about prospective stability for the next five years. I think that we have the prospect of other possibly quite dramatic changes, possibly in resources, maybe in the numbers game, maybe in sites, maybe in amalgamation. I can see that we could possibly have another five years in many respects not dissimilar from the period through which we have gone. Because the manner in which the changes have come about have contained so many impulsive or else undisclosed acts of policy which have had to be inferred that one cannot feel confident that those who are making the policy may not be equally impulsive or may not be ready to take certain actions the motivations for which are as concealed as the ice that the Titanic struck.

This uneasiness is intensified by some of the remarks in the papers prepared for the Brighton Conference. I think David Hencke quite rightly makes the point that the thrust whereby policy is being developed has not been essentially academic. One must, of course, recognise that there are other factors in this equation besides questions of academic or pedagogic purity. Nevertheless it is incumbent upon us not to sell the pass on things that we do consider to be educationally essential. And we have not even been given the time ourselves to develop a coherent statement of what we do consider to be academically and educationally essential. The decisions have proceeded essentially, as David Hencke suggests, from politicians and civil servants.

Their motivations are related to logistic matters, to finance, sites and structures. No one (with all respect to the James Committee) has consistently said 'our motivations are to secure the best teacher education we can, given our national resources'. Teacher education has been treated as a residual byproduct of a series of games that are being played by other rules and for other reasons. Bill Percival makes the same point in his discussion paper. Everybody knows that, while very good work has been done by many college staffs under conditions of great difficulty in the course of the last two years, they have done it in a time when far too much of their energy has had to go into their own career problems and the problems of their colleges - more energy than they have ever devoted to such topics in their lives. One ought to pay tribute to the mass of college staffs who have shouldered a very heavy additional, and for some of them unusual, unfamiliar work load, coping meanwhile with the problems of dealing with their students and maintaining their normal academic obligations. But I think they have felt that they are being asked to contribute academic formulae, formulae for new degrees, formulae for new structures, without the possibility of an adequate discussion among themselves; they have had to sit in committees making academic decisions while all the time they have had to look over their shoulders at all sorts of internal power plays between departments, and so on. They have not been able to undertake this task in what one would consider a genuinely intellectual climate. It has in fact been undertaken in a climate of anxiety, indeed, in many cases, of profound anxiety. And also in a climate in which, for a variety of reasons which lie outside the control of the colleges, and of the universities in many respects, they have not been able to involve the profession for whom we are training people in a significant way in those debates.

We have done what we can in the Sussex ATO to involve representatives of the teaching profession at all levels in discussions about new awards and new structures but the teachers themselves are grappling with their own problems, with their own anxieties about changing in-service provision, school organisation and curricula. In the past teachers have not been adequately involved in that level of professional debate, now, in an emergency situation, it has been difficult to suddenly bring them into that debate and give them an opportunity to express themselves effectively. One of the major problems in the next five years is how to involve practising members of the profession in our problems, not only the problems of actual classroom practice and all the things that go with that but how to involve them in our curricula and educational debates in a way that we do not lose contact with them. There are very grave dangers in considerable areas of this country of effective contact being lost with members of the profession.

All this means that a series of vital questions have hardly been raised at all, or raised only in conferences and private negotiations in which teachers have scarcely been represented. For example, I do not believe the question of size, which is a far more critical question than is often realised, has ever been properly discussed. What is in fact a proper size for an institution in which teacher education occurs? The more I think of this question of size the more I am convinced that, in the search for economies of scale, or range of resources, or whatever it may be, we are seriously overlooking some of the major sociological and psychological implications of size. It is at least an open question whether there are not some kinds of student entrants going into some parts of the profession where the pastoral and other aspects of a relatively small college will be better than the results of being in a very large college. This may well be true of many primary teachers, for instance. I don't see why we should not try to preserve at least a fair range of diversity of sizes and types of college and allow people some choice. Five hundred teacher places in a polytechnic may produce quite different responses and may indeed even affect the type of student who is attracted to teacher training by the nature of that institution. Professor Stern, of the University of Syracuse, did a lot of work about ten years ago on what he called 'the attractive image' of institutions of higher education. He found that each had its own profile; that the 'image' was almost like a self-fulfilling prophesy that tended to attract certain types of student. We do not know whether a policy which in effect destroys certain types of college may not cut off the flow of certain types of student. I feel that we have to ask two basic questions: What is the contribution of the small college? And what is the effect of the large college?

Next - and I think this is where we are all in the dark - what is the impact of diversification? We have all talked a lot about diversification over the last year or so. I think I know what it means broadly enough; I think I know what we have got to try and do about it. What are the implications? Start, if you like, with the staff who have got to achieve different kinds of input and different kinds of response. Consider the feelings and problems of the students in an institution where diversification is taking place. We are all guessing about the effects. Let me just give you a very quick example of what happened at the University of Sussex in the early days. Many people came to Sussex who were historians, philosophers, sociologists, and so on but in many of the courses that we developed, however, people found themselves teaching at the interesting and cross-disciplinary edge of their subject, not in the mainstream of the discipline. This produced much stimulating work - and a considerable degree of professional frustration later on. It created intellectual problems, teaching problems, problems of examination - even of the future careers of the students involved. We know far too little about diversification in this sense; it could easily end in producing a flashy educational supermarket, in which everything is neatly packaged and there isn't a square meal (in both senses!) in sight.

Then, to open another set of issues, how can we begin to discuss the whole range of questions which arise when we link teacher training institutions with polytechnics. Now I am not saying there is no teacher training in polytechnics - of course there is - our own Polytechnic here has been a member of the ATO ever since we were established. But I think that there is a very significant difference, let us say, from the academic board level downwards when you are beginning to argue priorities, resources, academic pay, in an institution where the main weight has not been in teacher education. Some of these differences may be positive. For example, when we consider what one might call community links, sandwich-type courses and experience-related courses, polytechnics may well have more to offer than universities and monotechnic colleges. One shouldn't underestimate the kind of contribution they can make if they can formulate this in the right way.

Another question which seems to me to raise a whole range of ideas is the matter of student reaction. Where do students want to go? Will some potential teachers now be lost? Will others, new to the profession, choose to go into teacher education? How will students react to an institution which has been amalgamated or linked with a polytechnic where teacher education is only a part of it and not the central purpose. Above all, what is going to be the student reaction when, as course co-ordinators or validators, or whatever it may be, we design nice structures with modular arrangements where, if the DES wants more teachers or less teachers, we move students this way, close this door, open that door? So that it begins to look like the demon coming out of the pantomime traps. What will actually happen to the students who will be shuffled through these yes/no gates? One of the papers suggests that the consecutive idea designed for a quite different situation, will not work in a situation in which the entry into teaching may for a variety of reasons become more favoured. Or it could work the other way. There may be indefinite postponements and really confused programmes, as students try to keep their options open.

We have talked about enlarging choice; it has been a major objective of policy. I am in favour of widening choice as far as is possible - but I think we may be widening choice to the point where choice will not be the student's decision, or even the student's tutor's decision, but the result of logistic pressure and other quite impersonal factors.

Another range of issues derive from the question: how will the new institutions be managed? Polytechnics are managed in a rather different way and they are bigger institutions than most colleges of education. Most colleges of education have been run, I think it is fair to say, on what one might call the see and talk model; in other words, the Principal could see most of the staff most of the time and settle issues informally and quickly. Polytechnics, I think it is fair to say, are not on the whole see and talk. They tend to develop almost as heavy top level echelons as universities. How you actually argue the educational academic syllabus, problems of teacher education and all the other related professional problems in a polytechnic management structure as against the way they have been hitherto argued as a monotechnic structure is not beyond the wit of man to solve. But it will be a difficult problem to resolve - much time and many errors. The management, finance, resource allocation and other problems were hitherto solved largely for a college once it had its numbers - if it had a reasonable governing body and knew how to run itself. It is not going to be like that in the future; the new situation will involve the jostling of faculties and the matching of unlike claims which are familiar in polytechnics but new to college staffs. Some of the people who have been quite capably managing colleges of education will play their game in a different league in future. Can they successfully press the claims of teacher education?

There is a whole group of questions related to the quality of courses. The universities that will validate - and the CNAA - will have to reconsider what we mean by standards. How do we maintain them? Whose standards are we maintaining, by what criteria? Are we maintaining them by platonic standards or by what we think other people will accept at a given moment in time? Universities solved that problem in the past by the very simple device of saying that all men are equal but different, which is a very easy way of avoiding the question. Once you open the door to other people to start developing new degrees, new styles of teaching, you begin to discover the shaky assumptions upon which academic awards have been based historically. The question of validation is difficult enough when you are dealing with new courses; it's infinitely more difficult when you go beyond the syllabus and try to judge the quality of the teaching.

I have great doubts about either academic qualifications or research work being really good indicators as to whether somebody is a good teacher. What we usually say is that in the absence of any evidence, these criteria have to provide a rough judgement about the ability of a teacher in higher education - though we all know good teachers who have not got higher degrees and have not done much research. Once you start trying to translate these criteria into judgements about an institution, you are in the higher-guess-work. How can you say that the quality of a new BA in teaching compares with the quality of an existing B. Ed in teaching? It's a commonplace, repeated by the James Committee, that the quality of professional courses is not high. What does that mean? How, precisely, do we move from that general statement to a set of criteria you can use when you are actually with the people in the room who are teaching that course? We have got to find, I think, some kinds of performance specifications for some of our tasks which will allow at least a little more objectivity.

Lastly, in this sort of catalogue of problems, I want to draw your attention to one area which I feel is very important. It came up in the whole debate over the launching of the B. Eds, which has inevitably got pushed aside; and will, I think, come back very strongly. What is the relationship between pre-service and in-service courses and methods of teaching? When the in-service B. Eds first came in there was a great deal of discussion whether they needed new courses, or whether they should be assimilated into existing B. Ed courses. In some cases this had to happen, in some cases it ostensibly happened; but there were many people (and I was one of them) who argued that the assumptions and content and teaching methods for people who are already in the profession are not necessarily the same and in some cases may be vastly different from those of pre-service students.

When you move into any kind of modular and diversified system you face a similar problem. What is suitable for whom? As we are going to have, not only in teacher education but probably in other areas as well, increased numbers seeking some kind of post-service or in-service awards or at least experience, the relationship of those two in curriculum building, staff allocation and so on, seem to me to be vitally important. On this matter at least, we have been left a degree of freedom, so that we can make up our own minds without worrying too much about logistic problems, sites and so on. It is a genuine internal academic question capable of resolution in our own terms in our own houses. I think it is one that will prove to be most important and will have a bearing on a whole range of other issues.

I have been briefly noting some of the issues we need to turn our minds to. The other comments I want to make are in a slightly different dimension. I have been critical of the present situation and its tendencies - of the desperate struggle to make sense and to survive the changes thrust upon us, but I feel that I must add that there are some positive aspects in our situation. First, diversification and increased flexibility, for instance, must bring benefits as well as troubles. We have been too rigid in our conception of the context as well as the content of teacher education. Secondly, the broadening of the polytechnics must be a good thing. The polytechnics have themselves been too monotechnic in many respects, but they have had problems, not only resources problems, in extending their range, and these changes must, in the long run, be for the general good of those institutions and the students in them. Thirdly, it must, in many cases, be a change for the better if teacher education occurs in new institutions with more and more varied resources. Fourthly, I welcome in general terms, although I am uneasy about some aspects of it, a move towards intermediate and transferable awards. I have long regarded the rigidity of our non-transfer system as a major source of waste and frustration in the system. Transferability should be a major concern of public policy in higher education. We cannot otherwise seriously begin to talk about major reforms in the structure of our system. Fifthly, I think the opportunity to revise academic structures, curricula and so on, is to be welcomed.

These points, however, are not limited to teacher education, for they apply to higher education as a whole and are a by-product of other changes rather than of a reform in the education of teachers. What we are seeing is the emergence of something much closer to the American structure, though it seems to me without some of its advantages. We are creating a number of new institutions which may loosely be described as Intermediate Colleges. That is, a kind of college which will be neither monotechnic teacher education institutions, polytechnics nor universities.

It may become something very like the four-year college which is familiar in the United States. I actually like the four-year college. I think it serves a very real role in the United States and I think many people gain a great deal from its existence, for it appears to provide a crucial step - not to equality of educational opportunity - towards a viable and sensible gradient of opportunity. I don't think one wants all institutions the same. I think what one wants is the ability for a person who has got certain capabilities to go on to an institution that suits them and from which they can benefit. At the point where they are capable of going somewhere else, up, down or sideways, they should be able to make that move. In other words, it is a student-based system and not an institution-based system. The existence in the United States of the universal high school diploma and general currency for credit hours or awards achieved elsewhere provides the absolutely essential underpinning for such a system. That is why the whole question of transferability is central to the debate of the next ten years. But of course, if one starts talking about a three- or four-year college of this kind, which grows out of an original sort of base in teacher education (and one must remember that quite a number of American colleges did in fact grow out of exactly that base themselves) one realises that we are talking about the emergence of a new kind of institution in which teacher education is one of its ancillary functions, though it may be one of its originating functions. We are talking about institutions in which the primary purpose is not the education of teachers but in which the education of teachers is part of some other set of social and educational objectives.

Nobody, so far as I know, has thought through the consequences of this development, though it may turn out in the long run to be the most important by-product of the present changes. Has there been any serious investigation of the nature and problems of the four-year

American college, and the bearing it has upon our own plans? Have we considered at all how it will relate to the rest of the higher education system? And where are these colleges going to look for academic support in the immediate future? To universities? To polytechnics? To the CNAA? Will they be left to struggle as best they can, or can we devise something constructive to replace the much-maligned - but, at their best, much valued, ATOs? Can we look forward to clusters of colleges which relate to other institutions of post-secondary education - not merely for validation but more importantly for the kind of academic encouragement and assistance they will need? How much time has been spent at Elizabeth House, or anywhere else, considering how new regional relationships will develop and what they should be like? To ask such questions is at present to get some dusty answers. And yet the future prospects of the staff and students of such colleges may well depend upon the answers we can find.

What applies generally to these new types of college of course applies specifically to teacher education. Where will the focus of professional interests lie? How will the teachers be involved? How will standards be set? Where will the dialogue about the nature of teacher preparation and in-service education take place - and how will we feed in the results of experience as well as research? And how far will educational as well as management decisions about teacher training be made by bodies whose members may not have much knowledge of its problems. Surely, if some kind of regional support cluster will be needed to sustain the stresses of diversification, a similar structure will be needed to ensure that teacher education does not degenerate into a muddle - to save us from going backwards while, publicly, everyone insists that we are going forwards. The answer does not lie in merely devising neat organisational plans. It lies in preserving and extending relationships. As matters stand, the relationships built up by years of association and joint endeavour have been badly strained. Some were bad, and ought to go; others were good, and rewarding, and must be preserved. In Sussex, and in many other

ATOs, I am sure, we have a degree of mutual understanding and confidence between the ATO members which has been personally pleasant and professionally rewarding. I would hope we can preserve that confidence and the practical working links that sustained it.

There is a further question which I will only mention. How can those engaged in teacher education in the new institutions turn a more encouraging face to the communities in which they live and work? All of us who have had anything to do with in-service work know how good it is for us and how we enjoy it; one of the things that keeps one alive is people who are coming to do in-service B. Eds., diplomas and higher degrees. What one gets out of it is a variety of ideas and interchange which is exciting, pleasant and rewarding. We have to extend that range of activity beyond teacher education, to social work and community problems and other vocations, to use those who are already involved in life and have professional competences and experience in our work. They can contribute something that we ourselves cannot offer our students. The whole question of new involvements, of the external teacher consultant, professional tutor, etc, seems to me absolutely vital in the next five to ten years.

I have asked enough questions. Perhaps the fact that we can ask so many questions is the most hopeful aspect of the present upheaval. But in searching for answers that may make the new institutions viable, may assist diversification, may create new educational possibilities, let us not forget our primary obligation - to prepare teachers and to assist those who are teaching. What I fear is that this obligation has got pushed down very low on the agenda of issues which we have to face in the next three years.

# The Changing Structures

The design of the Conference was to start from a review of the structural change process and then move on to consider curriculum change factors, especially major issues such as validation and modularity, concluding with a look to the future. Norman MacKenzie set the scene by suggesting that the changes in teacher education have escalated in a manner not to be foreseen five years ago. Although 'change' was proposed, its scale and impact were not prescribed in detail and indeed each year the process has become more drastic and swiftly moving. And each year the anxieties rise as the personal position of each and every member of college staffs is seen to be some degree at risk. As Professor MacKenzie rightly says this does not make for a 'genuinely intellectual climate'.

In this section David Hencke's analysis of the decision-making process for college re-organisation is hard hitting and perceptive. Although to an extent his contribution is time-specific in that it details and cites a changing situation, the lessons to be learned are clear. Those who week by week have scanned The Times Higher Educational Supplement for some inkling of their future and that of their colleagues in other colleges will find the article has few surprises for them. David suggests that a major re-organisation of higher education has taken place in secret in an ad hoc fashion, and that time has come for a new policy for this 'confusing world'. Now, he argues, is the time for decisive and democratic policy-making if we are to avoid making the same mistakes again.

James Porter in his article balances the factors that have brought about change - economic stress, falling birthrate, apparent falling demand for higher education places, lost opportunities in the sixties for colleges to institute change on their own account, and a general climate critical of teacher education institutions - and suggests that the future of teacher training lies in a smaller number of centres. He fears that the opportunity for colleges to really diversify in an imaginative way will be lost and that present trends indicate that what is desperately needed now is a period of consolidation so that a policy for integrating teacher education into higher education can be developed in a more organised manner. Finally he argues that teacher education needs to acquire its own academic and professional base in order to sustain it within the larger institutions in which it will take place.

Alec Ross considers the relationship between universities and colleges and argues in the first instance for retaining a small number of monotechnic institutions where the corporate identity of teacher training can be preserved. He proposes the establishment of a handful of university or polytechnic colleges of education with symbiotic relationships with their partners. These new institutions should be seen as 'centres of excellence' which would be of international stature in many ways including research in pedagogy and which would set standards for all teacher education. The structural changes have come at a very inopportune time. The LEAs are economically hard pressed but anxious to retain control, and the students for the colleges are no longer appearing in as great numbers. In the new institutions there will be no surplus of resources to ease transition, and the building of new relationships with the sixth formers and with future employers will be made more difficult by the awareness of both that new jobs for young teachers will be severely reduced in the next decade. No certain post will await a newly qualified teacher and no sixth former in assessing the value of higher education in this area will forget this.

# The re-organisation of the colleges of education: a critical overview

## David Hencke

The last two years I have been given the task of monitoring the future of teacher education on a week by week basis in The Times Higher Education Supplement. Over this period I have gradually become more appalled, not so much at the result of re-organisation which could conceivably have been predicted, but by the whole decision-making process which has surrounded this period of rapid change. Naively, having studied British Constitution at school at 'A' level, and a little less naively, having taken a joint-honours politics course at university, I have come, after observing government in practice, to the sad conclusion that the emperor has indeed no clothes. Indeed, I wonder if he ever deluded himself in the first place. What I intend to do in this article is to analyse, at at least attempt to, what has actually happened. I shall start by looking at the three major documents connected with re-organisation: the James Report, the 1972 White Paper and Circular 7/73. I shall also comment on the fourth, the recently published Reports on Education No 82. I shall then attempt to analyse the roles and influence of the various groups involved in re-organisation and, finally, offer perhaps a few ideas on how the debate should go from here, and what preventative medicine, because I think preventative medicine is necessary, is needed to stop this happening again. I need not go into the history of the James Report: it is probably better known to you than to me. But if one is looking at the document from the point of view of re-organisation - it is essentially the academic case for change.

The report was chaired by an academic - Lord James; its committee was staffed mainly by academics; it visited academic institutions, and took most of its evidence from academics. Its proposals highlighted the perennial problem surrounding teacher education courses - the need to have a high standard of personal academic education plus first-class professional training to become a qualified teacher. It led the way for the Diploma of Higher Education - on a broad enough base so that both the courses at Berkshire and NELP, different as they are, essentially draw from the same document. It raised the possibility of colleges seeking validation for degrees outside universities, leading later to involvement of the CNAA, at a time when the colleges were completely dominated by the universities. It suggested the idea of an expanding liberal arts college, and, finally, proposed the James cycle of initial induction and in-service training. But also, and this is now largely forgotten in the storm of protest that followed this report, it proposed a new administrative structure for the colleges, which would keep teacher education as a separate but equal part of higher education.

If I may quote from The James Report, Chapter 5 it emphasised two points. One that the links of the universities with teacher training would be those of an open partnership of institutions of higher education, and two, that the schemes proposed would bring together in a concerted working relationship in each region the professional institutions. That is, the colleges of education, plus the departments of education in the polytechnics and universities, together with a separate representation of all universities and polytechnics in the region, all the local authorities, the teachers in the schools and further education establishments.

Now, if one turns to the White Paper of 1972 - the immediate change I notice is that the academic argument has shifted from the academics to the politicians and the civil servants. From this point the power of academics who were consulted fully before the paper was produced, are removed - and they have never been re-instated since. The reorganisation of colleges, which was originally suggested in James solely for academic reasons, now becomes purely a question of politics and economics. From this point teacher education joins the so-called 'family of higher education' - it becomes part, according to this document, of a dispensable resource that can be moulded to meet the demands of that well-known Whitehall phrase, the so-called 'non-university sector of higher education'. Now how does this transition happen? It happens in two stages. Section 11 of the White Paper marks the end of one chapter of the James proposals for administrative change. Instead of a consolidated role of colleges in one group - the four functions suggested by James are hived off; academic validation is hived off to the CNAA or the universities instead of to a single body; professional recognition as the White Paper suggested will be accepted, but only in general principles, with no detailed commitment; in-service training has been accepted but not yet implemented, and in fact, the discussion on in-service training seems to be centred round private papers and not publically debated; and finally, higher education supply which is described as development, financial support and control of higher education institutions now becomes part of what is a chaotic system of polytechnic and other further education controls. At this stage the government is abandoning the re-organisation of teacher training for the re-organisation of the public sector of higher education. Teacher education now becomes the problem of the 'planning and co-ordination of the non-university sector'. What under James was to be unified and consolidated now becomes fragmented to serve the economic needs of other sectors.

No more clearly is this outlined than in sections 16 - 18 of the White Paper, the second and final stage of this transition. At this point the familiar economic facts of the declining birth rate, the sign of a plateau in student demand comes into play; the familiar paragraphs which I know you all know well (145-147 and 152-153) show institutional changes must meet the economic circumstances of the times. If you just read this you see in 145 - 'In the planning of expansion there are three sets of considerations, far from easy to reconcile, to which the Government attach great importance. The first concerns the concentration in some areas of very large numbers of students on a scale which represents acute problems of residence or transport.' In other words, this is not academic. 'Many cities have within or near them, as well as a university and a polytechnic, one or more large colleges of education. This will lead the Government to question any proposal that in this context a college of education should be expanded to form a separate third centre.' This is not academic, it is economic. And the same is even more stressed in paragraph 146: 'A second, opposite, consideration is that an institution capable of providing higher education courses adequate in standard and range must reach a critical size to obtain full economies of scale'; and it continues, as you know, setting a limit to the number of further education colleges, etc. But as you see, it is clear that the arguments are not necessarily academic.

This section also marks a turning point in a further transfer of power, this time from the wider world of politics and economics to detail planning. In other words, just as the academics were removed from the centre of the debate at the time of the White Paper, Circular 7/73 marks the transfer of power from politicians to administrators. This Circular specifically deals with sections 16-18 of the White Paper which also gives power to local authorities 'to consider in the light of local circumstances in what detail their plans should be prepared. But at the same time, as the DES acknowledges, that local authorities can do this, it also acknowledges that they were not in a good position to do it. 'The timetable for this process presents serious difficulties. The major re-consideration of the future role of institutions . . . and the extensive consultations . . . would even in favourable circumstances confront some authorities with a formidable task. The fact that this must be undertaken in a year when they are pre-occupied with all the problems arising from local government re-organisation adds to the difficulties.' (Circular 7/73, paragraph 8). This, although local authorities have delegated powers, the DES, which is not in the throes of re-organisation, can afford to make 'suggestions' which the local authorities cannot refuse.

Finally, there is the new DES Report on Education No 82, published in March 1975. Again, although this begins with a ministerial statement, which is clearly put at the front of the report, the entire document is an economic, manpower planning, and administrative exercise. Parliament, while being informed of thirty colleges being closed, is not even told the following points:

1. New entrants on initial courses will be reduced from 30,000 to 12,000 by 1978 and subsequent years.
2. Four-year courses to rise from 17 per cent to 40 per cent by 1980.
3. One-year courses for postgraduates to rise from 5,000 to 7,500 in 1984.
4. In-service places in colleges reduced from 15,000 target in the White Paper to 12,000/13,000.
5. New details on wastage from courses and married women returners is affecting the figures.

This document thus represents, in my view, the prima facie case of power passing to the administrators. Now, not only is detailed planning covered by civil servants, but the White Paper itself is partially rewritten without informing Parliament of the details. And the only way one can find out is by looking on page six, right bottom corner, tucked away, at the figures. (They are a long way away from the Ministerial Statement, which is right at the front.)

The conclusion of this part of the analysis shows how academic plans suggested by James become economic and political considerations and a policy of a very different kind emerges in practice. We now have to look at the implementation of the schemes in the last two years. What has happened is that within two years of the publication of Circular 7/73 a rapid re-organisation scheme has been initiated, not only affecting the future of the training colleges, but the whole of the public sector of higher education. This picture is now, barring the last details, almost complete. It affects not only the one hundred and fifty colleges, but possibly another hundred institutions in one way or another, from further education institutions to universities and polytechnics. The result is that teacher training places are being reduced from 114,000 in 1972 to 58,500 by 1981. Of these, initial teacher training places are unlikely to be more than 40,000; one-year postgraduate places about that time about 6,000 and 12-13,000 in-service places.

Institutionally, 30,000 places have been taken out of colleges and put into the polytechnic development programme. They are allowed under the scheme to turn over 15,000 places for further/higher education, and keep 15,000 for teacher training. 15,000 will remain in monotechnics, and 30,000 in liberal arts colleges and colleges of further and higher education. Some 14,000 places are being lost entirely by closures. Universities are mopping up about 4,000 places. The distribution is now fairly clear following the Government's August 1975 circular. It seems that thirteen colleges at least are to be closed; just over forty will merge with twenty-five polytechnics, six with universities (Coventry and Loughborough are proceeding and negotiations are continuing with St Luke's and Exeter University; Llandaff and University College, Cardiff and St Mary's and Bangor Normal and the University College of North Wales). Just over twenty are expected to remain monotechnic or mainly monotechnic and fifty colleges will become institutes of higher and further education by merging with each other (Eastbourne) or with further education colleges (Bradford). In addition a small number will become institutes of higher education in their own right, like Berkshire.

From an analysis of decision-making, the pattern of re-organisation appears to be as follows. First, the safeguarding of isolated monotechnic colleges to keep what the White Paper called the geographical distribution of higher education places. Thus there were minor cuts for North Riding, Scarborough and none for Charlotte Mason, although in fact Charlotte Mason had a strong case as an academic institution, it was probably saved because there was nothing else between Glasgow and Lancaster. Secondly, some safeguarding of liberal arts institutions, with the result that there will probably be limited cuts for Berkshire and Edge Hill, purely because the White Paper economics have now meant that there are going to be very few of these institutions. They obviously want to preserve one or two colleges and their preservation has probably come because they are so few, rather than as I can gather from any great academic criteria. The third point is the retention of monotechnics in some areas, which is the one thing that James wanted to break up. It now appears twenty will survive; for example, Madeley (against the original DES suggestion), Northumberland is likely to concentrate on teacher education, and Westminster College in Oxfordshire. Fourthly the large reductions in the polytechnic sector where more than one college is merged with a polytechnic. Best example of this is the decisions to merge Northern Counties and the City of Newcastle (itself a merged college) into the Newcastle Polytechnic, with a loss, I think, of about 1,200 places. Others may follow in Leeds, where it is likely that James Graham will disappear; in Sheffield the hint seems to be that Totley Thornbridge will disappear, leaving Sheffield with about 700 places, compared with 2,400 teacher training places previously. Birmingham is another possibility with three colleges being merged; Wolverhampton, particularly if Dudley, in addition to Wolverhampton Day and Wolverhampton Technical College, merges; and finally another good example will be Teesside where it seems that the DES economics really worked very fairly. In Teesside, incidentally, the college of education is a brand new college built in the 1960s for expansion, and is therefore likely to remain as a resource centre for teacher education for the polytechnic, whereas Middleton St George looks like being given the opportunity of either closing or being used as a Humanities Section for Teesside Polytechnic. As far as I can see, it has nothing to do with the strength of the colleges concerned.

The final, and saddest thing of all, the closure of thirteen or more of the colleges concerned The first five are Alnwick, Radbrook, Saffron Walden, Mary Ward and St Pauls. The next five seem likely to be the ones threatened last year, Putteridge, Bury, Endsleigh, Furzedown, Hereford and Wentworth Castle, Barnsley, which has the smallest intake of students for any college, eighty students a year for a 240 place college. This is likely to be followed, I understand, by discussions with the Church of England and Roman Catholic authorities, where Mr Harding will be going along to say 'Which colleges would you like to close?', with his eyes on Hockerill, Bishop's Stortford, Culham in Abingdon and, possibly, the college which in fact lost out by not going to Carlisle, St Peters, Saltley, Birmingham. Some of the closures could be caused by two colleges merging (for example, Doncaster and Scawsby) and teacher training being confined to one site. By closure, I would add, this means the end of initial teacher training in that institution. The DES has no power to actually close the colleges; all it does is withdraw the courses so that no-one can go there. Some of these institutions will continue to be professional centres (Alnwick) and offer adult education courses. Some will be used for comprehensive schools (Furzedown), and some (Mary Ward) will be sold and cease to have any connection with education. Now as far as I can gather there has been no academic rationale to this at all; and if we are to believe all we hear some of the dealings have been absolutely amazing. The latest rumour was that when Dennis Healey went to Saudi-Arabia to save the balance of payments he offered to throw in a couple of colleges of education, for training Saudi-Arabians in English. I think it was a necessity of the deal to find one in Hertfordshire which would be near to London for ease of access.

Now, having described the final changes, I want to analyse the whole method of their implementation. It is my view that this whole process has disturbing implications for a democratic society - not so much in the nature of decisions which are sad enough, but the way it has been done. With breath-taking speed far-reaching decisions have been taken, which alter the structure of higher education so that within two years after the last DES circular was issued, it is now too late to do a thing about it. We have just witnessed, without information or public debate, this re-organisation. I cannot emphasise enough, as one of a small number of journalists who have been reporting what has been happening, the total confusion of the last two years. It may be of interest to you, if you think you are in the dark, to imagine how it is for us. Apart from the official documents I have quoted, the changes of the last two years have been accompanied by an almost complete silence from the Department. The Department does not release a single Circular 7/73 decision to the Press or the public of its own accord The reasons that it gives, unofficially, is that the number of decisions it is making are too many, and require too much work to justify the small amount of public interest. It has made exceptions (Brighton and Coventry) which I will talk about later. But the main thing is the Department thinks it is not in the public interest or enough in the public interest to talk about a major re-organisation in higher education.

To cover the sort of surveys we ran in the Times Higher Education Supplement it meant a hundred to a hundred and fifty telephone calls. This was the only way we could get information on the changes taking place. Obviously in a scheme of this size and difficulty, human error did creep in and I did make some mistakes - and for those I apologise - but the only alternative was to write nothing, absolutely nothing. Eventually, only by lunching people at what one hoped was the right restaurant, and hoping they would be a little indiscreet, and virtually creating a nationwide network of 'spies', who would keep me informed on development, were we able to publish. And when we did publish the response was quite amazing. Mr Fowler told the House of Commons that I suffered from a conspiracy theory of history for publishing a factual account of what was happening; Sir Toby Weaver took the trouble to tell an educational conference that 'trigger happy education correspondents' were going around the country because we named Mr Hugh Harding as the DES co-ordinator in our newspaper. Finally, the late Stan Hewett devoted the front page of his own ATCDE communique to say the press was not always well informed on the issues, and advised members 'to examine carefully any press reports and not to place too much reliance on them'. It is intriguing to see the alarm caused in some quarters by the publication of detailed reports on the situation. It is also intriguing to see how people did not come forward to clarify the situation; they preferred to go in for 'press-bashing'.

However, to return to my main thesis, the only conclusion one can draw from the implementations of re-organisation is that the power, resources, ability and machinery lay within one group, the administrators, who not only were implementing but actually <u>initiating</u> decisions. The very last people to have any say on events were the college lecturers and students who were the very people most affected by the decisions being taken, and, the very people it was supposed to be all about. This took place in spite of the efforts of both the National Union of Teachers and the ATCDE. Of the two unions that were concerned, there is no doubt in my mind that the NUT took the stronger line, but it was virtually powerless to take any action, as it only had the minority of members in colleges. It did commission research from Manchester University (such as the document How Many Teachers), but it had neither the resources nor the manpower to offer more than a token opposition in isolated cases. Thus, if you compare the NUT's resources with the DES, with the College Re-organisation Committee, the links between Permanent Secretaries, between the DES, the Treasury and other Departments, and all the wealth of information they were getting from local authorities, you can see the efforts of the NUT were absolutely puny compared with what was going on. They had no alternative, but they did however get some things done. At one meeting of ACST, they were actually instrumental in getting some figures published. When it was suggested that the figures for teacher supply should remain confidential so that there could be no debate at all, the NUT threatened to make its own press release. The moment that was suggested everyone thought the release should be official! But the union could not produce an alternative policy that could meet the economic and resource based arguments (even if they couldn't be faulted academically) that was behind DES policy.

If we examine the ATCDE - the time and resources at its disposal were minimal compared with the magnitude and complexity of the problems it faced. In fact, it is even smaller than the NUT and has about six full-time staff. The late Stan Hewett had the educational ability (a senior civil servant said last week that his papers were some of the few that could be passed straight to a Minister) but he took the 'realist' approach. His achievement, one could say, was that he safeguarded his members' interest by getting good redundancy terms and by seeing that as many people as possible got new jobs in polytechnics and other colleges. Examining ATCDE policy, one only has to look at their executive statement last Oxtober to see what their attitude was. It said 'The current re-organisation is essentially a pragmatic exercise undertaken with due regard to local and regional circumstances. One's impression is that an enormous amount of flexibility is already being used. One can detect, within the broad lines of the White Paper policy, a quite remarkable variety of solutions.' The statement continues by saying that it cannot give automatic support to the aspirations of any particular college. It is clear that the ATCDE did not oppose the fundamental changes proposed by the DES, but how far did they welcome them? In May 1974 the late Stan Hewett gave a talk - a personal talk, I must emphasise, at a private conference at Coombe Lodge, on The Colleges of Education and Re-organisation. In it he warned - and this is an official account, so there can be no accusations of inaccuracy - that his own members would share 'a profound sense of shock that their established expectations would be so rapidly and radically changed. From this sense of shock stems a feeling of resentment and some bitterness. As a result people are having apparently irrational reactions, almost trapped into saying that they believe that nothing should ever change, a position they would hardly defend in normal circumstances'. He concluded by welcoming the changes - particularly the mergers with colleges of further education - 'the net result will be the exposure of teacher training. It will be open to comment and criticism by people not directly involved in it. The effect of these changes will be traumatic initially but salutary and productive in the long term. It will make us sharpen our professional and academic outlook and both further education, and colleges of education, staff will benefit. The staff of the new institutions will require a willingness and a capacity to live with a process of continuous change, and I would emphasise that bit. The institutions and the people within them must be able to adapt to changing needs and situations. There will not simply be one large adjustment to the new institutions. Therefore we have to think in terms of a constant process of staff adjustment, re-development and re-deployment within the institution, even if following the current re-organisation there came a wave of devolution there will be no return to the status quo, but the evolution of entirely different institutions. Therefore my final conclusion is that the status quo is officially dead - what is surprising is that we ever thought it could live'. Thus it could fairly well be said that the General Secretary of the ATCDE accepted both the economic and academic logic of the DES arguments.

If the unions were either powerless or agreed with the Department, what about the elected representatives in Parliament. The role of ministers in re-organisation plans appears to be confusing. Ministers are essentially busy men, and as the Crossman diaries show, they also have both political and departmental problems. Since re-organisation began we have had five ministers; two Secretaries of State (Mrs Thatcher and Mr Prentice) and three Ministers of State for Higher Education (Norman St John Stevas, Gerry Fowler and Lord Crowther-Hunt). Their influence on policy - in spite of two political parties which are essentially opposed - is in fact minimal. We have had the same consistent policy throughout. Yet the moment either Minister of State is out of office, he complains about the policy. Mr Hattersley, an opposition spokesman on education, promised to restore the teacher training cuts, yet Mr Prentice, despite the attacks on the Tories, implemented more drastic cuts this March than Mrs Thatcher would have dared in 1972. Mr St John Stevas, after initiating the White Paper with all its clear economic need for changes, took only four months to make the following speech to his constituency party (as reported in the Times Higher Education Supplement on 14th July): Headline: 'College shake-up is a disastrous mistake', says Norman St John Stevas.   Colleges of education should not be forced into shotgun unions with other educational institutions, Mr Norman St John Stevas, Opposition spokesman on education, told a meeting of his Chelmsford constituency association last week.   Mr St John Stevas was "very anxious about what is happening to our colleges of education".   Re-organisation was proceeding at an unseemly speed.   The government was making the same "disastrous mistake" with the colleges as with the grammar schools - destroying excellent institutions in order to achieve a formal uniformity. It was in the teachers' interests that the rate of expansion in the teaching force should be moderated, but at the same time, if quantity was reduced quality should be increased    "This will not be achieved by closing down colleges of education, which have traditions and personalities of their own, in an indiscriminate way", said Mr St John Stevas.   Re-organisation should take place only with the fullest consultation and the wishes of every college should be sympathetically considered.   Mr Prentice, the Secretary of State for Education, was using a bludgeon where a lamp was needed. He hoped Mr Prentice would moderate a policy which Mr St John Stevas likened to Henry VIII's dissolution of the monasteries.   Instead of disrupting colleges, the Department of Education should be looking towards means of improving professional training.   Potential teachers needed to be taught how to teach reading and mathematics in primary schools.

Backbenchers like Alan Beith, Christopher Price and Kenneth Clarke have tried to get information on particular decisions, but in most cases have not got an adequate reply.   If I may quote Hansard, when Mr Beith asked about Alnwick, he was told 'Of course the college isn't being closed, it is just a cessation of teacher training courses.   The Minister has not made up his mind,' etc.   It is rather interesting that when someone does try to raise something in Parliament they are just fobbed off.   Mr Beith definitely feels he was not helped.   I think he issued a statement where he made it clear how badly informed Ministers were.   I would at least have hoped that the civil service could have provided the Minister with up-to-date information.   The Minister mentioned a course in nursery training being contemplated by the college, when in fact it was already in operation. It seems very clear that people did not know what was happening.

The most interesting relationship is, however, between the role of the national civil service and the local authorities. There is no question in my mind, in spite of the delegated powers given to local authorities, that the main operation was a civil service operation - very much the national civil servant deciding the future with the chief education officer of every area - plus occasional national talks between voluntary bodies to keep them in line with emerging trends. Mr Harding, the Deputy Secretary responsible for re-organisation, made his priorities very clear at the same private conference at Coombe Lodge where Mr Hewett gave an address. He told them four interesting points:

1. That 'some of the solutions will have to be found nationally rather than locally, though others will have to be resolved at institutional level'. In other words 'If I don't like what the local authorities are doing, we'll do it ourselves'.

2. That the particularly important constraint in present economic circumstances is 'the most effective use of existing human and capital resources'. Where is the academic argument here?

3. That because of the need to make the best use of facilities and of the shortage of new capital provision over the next five and six years, we must expect there to be institutions which cater for both advanced and non-advanced work. Where is the academic argument that colleges of education and further education are going to benefit? Mr Harding says it is because of the need to make the best use of facilities.

4. That 'only the lucky colleges will find futures identical with the ones they would themselves have chosen. Others will have to accept less desirable compromises, assuming functions which they regard as less than ideal'. Practically everything he says is not based on academic reasons, it is purely a question of resources.

This resource-based policy was carried out either with or without the tacit support of chief education officers up and down the country over the last two years. Where chief officers disagreed with the DES the letters in response to the local authority proposals became rather abrupt. I have here a copy of a letter sent to Dr Briault on 3rd June 1974. Because Dr Briault disagreed with the cut-back and said he was going to use his delegated power to get what he wanted, the conclusion on the national situation is fairly clear. It says 'Finally, I need hardly emphasise the changing situation arising from the oil crisis and its effects on educational expenditure generally and on capital programmes in particular. It has already been necessary to defer a large number of capital projects for polytechnics and colleges and with the future so uncertain we must expect capital programmes to be strictly limited for some years to come. This consideration makes it all the more important that the valuable capital assets of our present colleges of education should be utilised to the full!'

Mr Harding had a few more abrupt words concerning Southlands, Whitelands, Digby-Stuart and Froebel colleges when they wanted to form Roehampton Institute of Higher Education. Mr Harding did not like the academic structure, so he told them: 'We fear that unless good progress can be made in this direction the decline in the need for teacher training places may make it necessary for one or more of the colleges to close by 1981. One must recognise in this context that they occupy sites with valuable development potential in an area of acute housing shortage.' I think that is rather intriguing, actually; I did not think Mr Harding cared about housing!

Now, if I may quote what happened to Northumberland when they dared to defy the Department, concerning Alnwick. The letter begins:

'Dear Trollope,

I explained we had regretfully come to the conclusion that for the following reasons we should have to recommend to the Minister the closure of Alnwick College:

1. The College is too small to diversify on its own.
2. The College is remote from other further and higher education institutions with which it might associate. (So is Charlotte Mason, interestingly enough.)
3. The quality of the College's intake is low. Although it nevertheless has achieved good results in the past, it had little or no chance of attracting one hundred per cent two A level intake.
4. If the College were to retain its initial training programme it could not be reduced significantly below its present size without endangering its overall viability. Its members can only be maintained at the expense of greater reductions in teacher training places elsewhere.
5. There was no indication that Newcastle University would reverse its decision not to validate the new three year B.Ed courses and all institutions would thus have to turn to the CNAA for validation. (The CNAA had not even been there, as I understand it. It is very interesting that Mr Harding could decide.)

Finally, if Alnwick were to retain the initial training function, it would only be serving as an appendange to the polytechnic in Newcastle, heavily dependent upon it for academic research.'

This was unlikely to prove a very healthy arrangement for Alnwick, especially since in the past its success had derived so absolutely from its independence!

We are supposed to think that it was not doing well enough to attract one hundred per cent students with two A levels! When we look at the other paragraphs, the way the DES can dismiss other colleges is quite amazing. The future of the remaining colleges, Northumberland, Northern Counties and St Mary's, Spenlowe, should be considered in relation to the polytechnic development.

'The intake of none of the colleges is strong academically. Northern Counties is about up to the national average while the other two are well below.'

A very interesting observation from a civil servant, and the intriguing thing is that Northern Counties was one of the first six to get CNAA validation, which is rather good for a college which can be dismissed in a sentence in a letter to Trollope.

> 'Finally,' he says, 'we see little prospect for all three of them in competition with each other, and with the Polytechnic developing B. Ed and other degree and diploma courses successfully with a two A level intake, the Polytechnic envisages an expansion of over 2,000 full time places.'

In other words, the colleges are being subject to what is the Polytechnic development plan. It has nothing to do with what they can or cannot offer and I think this is shown even more clearly in that Northern Counties which is the college which has achieved good academic results in teacher training, should be the one which has been pushed in and given this maximum reduction in teacher training places, whereas Northumberland, which was only planning its CNAA courses, has in fact been retained.

Even discussions at Elizabeth House began to get heated when the Church of England decided it did not really totally agree to amalgamations on a larger scale than anticipated. Someone very kindly sent me the minutes of the meeting at Elizabeth House - we can guarantee its accuracy - it was written by a civil servant! The Church of England objected to the idea of having to amalgamate every single college and a Bishop got rather annoyed. Mr Harding found this view out of line with previous statements of policy, and disturbing.

> 'It was accepted', Mr Harding told the Bishop, 'that the Church must contribute proportionally to the national reduction in teacher training places and if the Church insisted on the stronger colleges retaining their autonomy and independence, this was likely to be at the expense of closing perhaps five or six of the weaker colleges.'

In other words, whatever is said publicly about the autonomy of voluntary bodies, when it comes to the cruch in these private meetings, it is very clear who rules. But perhaps the most important of these examples are the new futures currently announced for Coventry and Brighton. In each case there was considerable opposition to the DES view - in one case, Coventry, opposed by the LEA; in the other, Brighton, supported by the senior civil servants in the LEA. These two cases illustrate the power of the civil service on the resources question; the role of the local authority and the lack of academic argument. In both cases the Department actually wanted a polytechnic-college merger. The results - a merger with the polytechnic in Brighton and a merger with the university in Coventry - were taken on resource allocations alone, not academic argument, and the only intervening factor was Mr Rendel Jones in Sussex and Mr Bob Aitken in Coventry, the two Chief Education Officers.

Talking to Mr Aitken a few days before this Conference, he explained how he was determined to have a university-college merger, in spite of a letter from the DES telling him, against his own local authority submission, that a polytechnic merger 'was in the interests of teacher education and a complementary academic development'. He described his negotiations as something much like a 'game of chess' with the Department. One main asset in the game was the resources available to Lanchester Polytechnic and the price of the agreement was simple. He told the DES that Coventry and Warwick would only agree to buy up St Pauls College, Newbold Revel, with a three hundred acre site, if the DES refused to force the college into the polytechnic. A university-college merger was won, not on academic reasoning, but on a land trading deal in the East Midlands. In Sussex, where the LEA agreed with the DES, the very letter saying that the Minister was reconsidering the arguments was headed to the Chief Education Officer with the fact that he could not be forced to sell his college to Sussex University. Here there were no easy sites to expand Brighton Polytechnic, no three hundred acre sites in Brighton to barter. Resources could be provided at a minimum cost by using the college campus. The local authority were behind the DES despite the fact that party whips had been on and the argument had been between the Labour and the Liberal Parties opposed by a Tory majority. And I think it must be said that privately a senior DES official admitted to me that this merger is not in the interests of teacher training but that the resources were needed to back up Brighton Polytechnic and it must be achieved at the minimum cost. The College buildings were built with 1960's money, so they are there and cheaper than 1975 prices. So, therefore, the resources argument has played a very, very important part, particularly where the link man, the chief education officer, agrees with the DES.

The conclusions I draw from all this is that there must be a better way of handling this sort of decision-making process than what has happened over the last two years. Let me say that I do reject some of the ideas of Dr Bibbly, Principal of Hull College, that the whole scheme was masterminded in secret by the DES - it was not. It appears more likely to be a whole series of haphazardly-made decisions done in the shortest possible time to achieve the cheapest solution. It may have been better indeed if there had been a national plan.

What is also clear is that what began as an academic operation to improve teacher training has now become the excuse for a re-organisation of a public sector on the cheap. The academic content, if it is there, has been buried below a whole series of resources calculations. It may be that there may have been no alternative open to people who had to take the decisions, for I think it is fair to say there had to be some cut-back in teacher supply. But it is fundamentally dishonest to pretend to people that this is basically an exercise to improve teacher training and courses for students. Basically once the White Paper was published, the Civil Service took advantage of fragmented opposition to push through a major re-organisation scheme.

What is needed is a new academic coherence to teacher education. I think we really need to build on the few innovations at Berkshire, Didsbury, Charlotte Mason, NELP and Lancaster, Sussex and Warwick Universities. We also need a new structure, so that academics, civil servants, politicians, local authorities, lecturers and students can have a dialogue, can plan together for the future. It is no good policy being handed down in tatty press releases or private meetings of a select few individuals while thousands of lecturers and academic boards plan syllabuses and futures that are meaningless to the current position and become wasted work. I think I have found nothing more depressing than going round college after college and finding piles and piles of academic work which will be completely wasted because people have not been informed. College principals who should have a good idea of the future of their colleges are often waiting for a hint from the staff inspector when he deigns to come round. This is an appalling way to carry out public policy. All educationalists should be better informed and if the system is made more democratic they will have to become more responsive to economic circumstances.

But a start must be made soon to change the structure of decision-making in higher education before another generation of students enters the confusing world that is the hallmark of the public sector of higher education. The Committee of Directors of Polytechnics actually state that running a polytechnic is an energy-sapping process because they have about nine or ten different constraints on them! I really believe we have to get down to making a new policy which is going to involve the academics, the politicians and civil servants, because if we don't, we are going to end up with another mess in a few years time, when we start playing about with regional higher education. The only thing that worries me is that I hope it is not too late to pick up the pieces from the confusing period of the last two years.

# Aspects of institutional change

**James Porter**

One of the main features in the current change in the institutional pattern of teacher training relates to its pace, comprehensiveness and range. This has been induced by reactions which vary from a determined attempt to pretend that nothing is changing at all along the continuum to what amounts to sheer panic. Whatever the picture as seen from the Department of Education and Science, the view from the level of the institutions has been confused and conflicting. The White Paper set forward a fairly clear policy line based fundamentally on the rapid reduction of numbers in teacher training. Two additional factors have, however, produced the present stressful and disturbing situation. They are the virtual collapse of the higher education expansion which was expected to absorb comfortably a substantial part of the teacher training system, and secondly the growing economic crisis. The strategy of the White Paper was inevitably linked to the assumption that applications for higher education would continue to increase. However, the link between the falling birthrate and the levelling-out of applications for higher education has seriously and dramatically affected the potential for higher education diversification in the colleges. Thus, colleges have been faced with a reduction on two fronts: an even more rapid run-down than was expected of teacher training numbers, and now a much more uncertain future in relation to higher education. The second factor, which has become increasingly dominant over the last three years, is the economic crisis. Underlying all discussions about institutional change is the nagging fear about the whole economy, and doubts about the country's economic viability over the next five years. Teacher training - because it is the only area in education to to fundamentally re-organised in the last two or three years - has been sucked into the economic crisis. Therefore, dramatic changes in institutions, talks of mergers and closures have taken place in an atmosphere where even more Draconian measures are being privately considered within the DES and within local authorities. The background is one in which severe economies have to be accepted in social services, in schooling and, indeed, in the whole public sector. The pressure is also upon universities, and higher education has difficulty in making its case against other apparently more urgent priorities.

Accepting that such factors have created the immediate 1975 situation, it must also be said that the history of the colleges of education provided them with little preparation for the scale and violence of the changes that they have undergone. Looking back over the last fifty or sixty years of teacher education one would see that until two or three years ago the pattern of teaching training that existed, and the institutions that served teacher training have remained relatively much the same over that period of years. The long, sustained pattern of teacher training has responded to various shifts, but these had been gradual and well contained institutionally. One looks, for example, at the pattern in the early 1920s, when there were some 67 training colleges in England: 48 of them were voluntary colleges, and so teacher training at that time was very much dominated by the churches and by the voluntary colleges. Up until the early '50s, in fact, the dominant influence in teacher training was that of the voluntary bodies. It is interesting to note that in those 48 colleges in the '20s none of them were mixed: 35 were women's colleges and 13 were men's colleges. There was a diocesan college here in Brighton in the 1920s, as well as the council college. Most colleges at that time had around 100 - 150 students. I myself joined a college some seventeen or eighteen years ago which was them one of the largest colleges in the country with 320 students. As a member of staff for five years, I remember only one or two new members being appointed over that period.

The length of courses had remained stable at two years for all students until the late '50s. There was a wide distribution of colleges over the country, and there was also established a close relationship with university departments of education. The major shift of the post-war situation was a change of balance from voluntary to local authority control of colleges. The massive growth in teacher training places after the war was mainly concentrated in the local authority controlled institutions, and the fact that now more than two-thirds of teacher training is in the hands of the local authorities continues to be influential in the way in which re-organisation has now taken place. The crude fact that the local authority owns the college and employs the staff is obviously a key factor when it comes to decision-making about institutional futures.

Until three years ago the vestiges of the old system were still very influential on the structure of teacher training: colleges were still monotechnic, and they were, of course, more typically co-educational because this had become the national policy. Another change, of course, had been the rapid growth in size. There was still, however, a sense of the colleges being a world of their own: people knew each other very well, HMIs were specially allocated to the colleges and, because both the Department and the colleges had a close interest in the development of schools, the relationship was a close and friendly one. Many important conferences were arranged through the joint sponsorship of the DES and the ATCDE. These conferences - particularly the ones on the teaching of education and professional training involving the education section of the ATCDE and the DES - had a profound influence on the development of educational studies and the interaction between theory and practice. The reputation of individual colleges was well known, and there was an almost closed system of interaction. The sixties could in many ways be regarded as a golden era for the colleges of growth, development and expansion, for, although people were groaning about the strain on resources, at least it was a period of excitement and change. It can also be seen now, looking back, as a period of missed opportunities.

In the early sixties the Robbins Report undoubtedly provided a false image of what might take place as a result of institutional development. Even at the time it seemed most unrealistic to propose that the colleges should become administratively and financially a part of the university system. It was unfortunate that a lot of people felt that Robbins was opening the door to a new relationship between the universities and the colleges. What, in fact, followed most significantly was the emergence of the binary policy during the latter part of the period of teacher training expansion. The binary policy was articulated in 1965 by Anthony Crosland at Woolwich, and colleges became the institutions most affected by the policy because they uneasily bridged the gap between the so-called autonomous and public sectors  The intention to provide for a balanced, separate but equal development in the two sectors has led inevitably to the transfer of the mass of teacher education to the public sector.

However, I want to argue that the major changes in the system have always been produced by demographic trends and the availability of resources. The growth, development and change in the sixties took place because of the increase in the school population, the injection of resources, of new staff, and a changed climate within the colleges through larger size. The unexpected birth-rate projections in the late fifties, coinciding with the three-year course development, were the major factors in producing this change: in other words quantitative factors were paramount. Concern regarding quality had been expressed for many years, and there have always been criticisms of the way in which we educate and train teachers, just as there have always been criticisms of the schools. Indeed, it would be a very odd society which found its institutions, its schools or its colleges satisfactory. If, for example, one looks back as far as the end of the nineteenth century, the day training colleges were set up in connection with the universities in the 1890s, as it was said at the time, 'to overcome the many serious disadvantages which the older colleges labour under, lack of adequate staffs, lower standards of intellectual training, insufficient facilities for practice teaching and especially the segregation which living in a separate institution necessarily involves'. In the 1920s the NUT argued that teacher training should be in three phases. (They did not use the term 'cycles' in those days!) General education through secondary schools should be satisfactorily completed; there should then be a three-year degree course and finally one year of professional training, during which the student could attain teaching craftmanship. Two-year training colleges, it was argued at that time, should be eliminated, and professional training should be school-based. The theoretical aspects of education should come later and not be compulsory at all during the initial stage. These arguments, these debates have been going on for a very long time.

The foundation of the current critique for the colleges rests upon the widespread concern about teacher training at the end of the sixties and the early seventies. Initial expression was given to this by the Special Select Committee of the House of Commons which went round the country in the late sixties like the old Congressional Committees in the United States, being highly critical of whatever it looked at, with backbench MPs getting at least a certain amount of press coverage. The last thing that the Select Committee looked at before it was dissolved with Parliament was teacher training. The Committee had, however, successfully established a highly critical mood, which led first of all to the Labour Party's response of setting up an ATO enquiry and then to the Conservative Government's establishment of the James Committee. However, it would be quite wrong to think that the setting for the current arguments is just something that has arisen over the last four or five years. This is something that has always been with us, and teacher training has always responded to demographic, economic and resource changes that have taken place, and to the argument and discussion about the quality and types of training. In view of the variety of users of the teaching training output - the schools, the public, parents, political groups - there will always be this debate, and there will always be a tension between the various members of the roles - set using teacher education. Such factors, therefore, represent the background to current institutional change. I have tried to argue that one must consider primarily the demographic and economic basis of the argument, and accept that the critique of the teacher training enterprise will be a continuing one.

We can now look briefly at the effects of all these changes on the internal structure of colleges. First of all, the response to the cutback in numbers in colleges was mild because of the encouraging tone and title of the White Paper. Colleges, after all, were still part of a 'framework for expansion', not for contraction. The severe economic setbacks following the White Paper, and the reduction of student targets were not apparent. Because of the assumed growth in higher education most colleges saw themselves in this new 'family'. Colleges had done a good job in the past in responding to the need for teachers; the numbers of students coming in with good qualifications were increasing, and staffs were young and active; resources were good. Why shouldn't they all become major institutions? However, as the small print was read more closely and local negotiations began, hectic activity - particularly in terms of new course designs - suddenly took over and led often to over-ambitious schemes. Utilisation of the maximum numbers of staff who were currently in post became a persistent element in the design. Certainly any curriculum relates to the abilities and resourcefulness of the staff who design them, but the increasing pressure to get such schemes validated often produced courses which were mere aggregations of what had gone before. Earlier syllabuses were sometimes chopped up into smaller 'modules' or units rather than the whole programme coming under concentrated scrutiny. B. Ed was all too easily superimposed on the new and much desired B. A. The grudging acceptance of two year's higher education for the Diploma, and the deep attachment to concurrence typified the unease that many colleges felt. There was a kind of withdrawal into a defensive posture on concurrence which limited the colleges' capacity to respond by genuine diversification.

However, as it became clear that amalgamation, rationalisation, closure and real re-organisation institutionally were upon us, there was an emergence of a greater realism. With a second wave of cut-back in teacher training and higher education, a whole range of different issues is being raised, and alternative institutional solutions are now being sought or enforced. The result has been an increasing emphasis on individual career future for staff in personal terms. It is important for internal academic structures to respond to this relatively new element. The old departmental structure, the unit which was based on the kind of teacher training that has not changed in a long time, is no longer appropriate for the new programmes or for course development based more clearly on individual staff initiatives. Thus, the growth of much larger academic structures within colleges is inevitable. 'Schools' or faculties give much more scope for flexible and co-ordinated planning. They also enable much more constructive co-operation to take place between different institutions.

What is desperately needed now is a period of consolidation for those engaged in the radical changes implied by the reduced teacher training numbers and the demands of diversification. A period of five years with firm teacher training output targets can give an opportunity for much more organised, well developed policy integrating teacher training and higher education. It can allow for staff development and retraining, and for sensible proposals carefully designed to lead to diversification at different levels. The particular contribution of the college, in co-operation with the LEA, and the establishment of a regional base growing from existing connections with the schools all need time to evolve. The setting up of the new Regional Consultative Councils can provide a helpful context for such development. One must face the fact that this will lead to a more favourable staff student ratio during the replanning phase. However, this ratio should still not need to be lower than the one currently operating in polytechnics. An overall target ratio of 1:10 by 1981 seems reasonable.

I should like to turn in conclusion to the implications of current changes for the future. Firstly, the location of teacher training must now be radically reconsidered. In the future I take the view that we need to have perhaps as few as fifty - and it may be even fewer - major centres of teacher education. We currently have something like 180 centres if one counts the polytechnics, universities and the colleges. The reason why it is necessary to reconsider a major reduction in the number is that teacher training must have a substantial part of any institution for it to have a proper share of resources and for it to have its proper impact on the institution itself. In view of the fact that it is generally accepted that teacher training should be part of higher education, the institutions in which it is offered should be recognisably institutions of higher education. In such circumstances fifty centres would seem to cope with the current numbers proposed, with centres of teacher education of between 600 and 1,000 places for initial and in-service training. We obviously have to stop talking about 'colleges' which are involved in teacher education and training, and talk about 'centres' for teacher training. Such centres will not be the total institution, and teacher education cannot any longer influence the total life of the institution. The implications of moving away from the monotechnic institution are profound for styles of teacher training. Hitherto teacher training arose from the total life-style of the college. It was considered that the important things that happened to a student often took place outside the lecture room and it was the total experience of three or four years at the institution that really mattered. The situation in future is going to be very different. The curriculum has got to be defended, and teacher education has got to stand alongside other courses within a much larger diversified institution. They need to be much more concerned with styles of learning and teaching.

Of course, the reduction in the number of centres arises from an acceptance of the target of 12,000 entrants by 1978. The evidence for this figure now seems as conclusive as it is ever possible to be in such projections. Indeed, if anything, the figures still seem optimistic. So one must think radically if one wants to have a significant size of centre of teacher education. If the staff, resources and the whole interaction of teacher education with the higher education establishment are important, then the number of institutions involved must be severely limited.

The other possibility which has now become quite clear is that of genuine interprofessional training. This has always been dismissed as being an unreal hope because numbers in other professions would be trivial compared with teacher training numbers. However, as teacher training contracts, the balance seems more even. If we are talking about 40,000 places for initial training, we are probably talking of something like 10,000 to 15,000 for social work and allied professions, if youth, community, health and the various levels of social work are included. Therefore, one should be looking very much for schools of social and teacher education, and bringing these to the forefront in terms of discussion, because the wider the professional interests of those involved in teacher education, the better. Clearly there is the danger of teacher education becoming a little enclave within larger institutions, isolated from what is happening because it does not have any bridge with other areas. The wider spectrum of interprofessional training would provide this more substantial base.

In-service training also urgently needs treachers to be working alongside other professionals: otherwise the in-service education of teachers could be as isolated as initial training has often been. One could diversify initial training and continue to isolate in-service training for teachers. However, the links between the social services and education, and between schools and outside agencies are being increasingly emphasised. They can often be seen most clearly by those who are actually involved, and this development can be carried forward by genuinely interprofessional in-service training. If one looks at what is happening in secondary education, the severity of the problems which many urban secondary schools are facing inevitably involves the other services, and alternatives to schools (for example, 'sanctuaries') are often manned by social workers. Many local and regional problems, as well as individual difficulties of various professionals can only be solved by the deepest co-operation. This must be sustained by genuine interprofessional training at both the initial and in-service stage.

The new situation, enabling us to concentrate attention on courses rather than the total institutions, should also lead to greater concern with professional formation. Such professional formation will depend increasingly on the schools, upon the effects of the 'practice' situation, and upon the school field-work. This is the sandwich work in teacher education which has often been neglected and unscrutinised. It is in the field that professional formation is most clearly going to take place, built upon a relevant and demanding phase of higher education in the college, and sustained by joint professional teams from school and college.

The final point to be made - and about which David Hencke had much to say, and which by implication Norman Mackenzie did as well - relates to power and control and future developments in this field. It must be hoped that this conference can begin to formulate ideas for a well organised, national assocation of teacher education concerned with both initial and in-service training. It is clear that there is a need for a coherent, sustained and authoritative voice for teacher education which is concerned centrally with the teacher education activity and not just with institutions in which teacher education takes place. In future, teacher education will have to be sustained academically and professionally as an area of activity rather than as a set of institutions which reflect it. This is the great change that is taking place. Just as medical education cannot just be the schools of medicine, and accountancy, legal training and architecture must be seen as something more than the institutions writ large, so in future, teacher education has got to have its own academic and professional base, its own argument. This requires over the next few years a coming-together of those whose central interests are in teacher training. I am not sure whether this should be part of a possible council of higher education, or whether it should be something separate from it. My feeling at the moment is very much towards the latter, because the roots of teaching are, of course, within the schools, and the professional future of our students is within the school setting. The involvement of professionals from within the schools would seem to be vital. After all, this combination of teachers and teacher educators on the regional bodies will have two-thirds of the votes, but will not have two-thirds in the influence if they remain divided. The importance of this co-operation, nationally, regionally and within the teacher education centres, is perhaps the most important step to be taken. This article has concentrated particularly upon positive outcomes from the sustained trauma of re-organisation which is only too pressing and immediate at this time. Another outcome may ultimately be encouraged: the commitment of a reduced but still significant number of professionals from schools, colleges, universities, local authorities and the DES working together on a coherent teacher education policy may ultimately show the need for a more comprehensive coherence in higher education itself. This may even help to dissolve, for example, that binary line which runs along the A. 27 between Brighton College of Education and the University of Sussex.

# Universities and colleges

**Alec Ross**

The words 'university' and 'college' are terms of great and ancient significance in the story of the development of higher education in Britain.   Though this paper is presented in the context of a Conference devoted to the consideration of problems arising at the present time from the re-organisation of teacher education, I shall nevertheless begin by considering the impact of these terms in higher education generally in the hope that at a time of radical re-structuring we might yet find in our tradition elements of continuity which could still serve us well.

We are all familiar with the idea of the college as it has developed in the ancient universities.   Few have ever dared to doubt the value of the collegiate structure in that setting and as those universities have grown in size the case for their colleges has become even stronger.   When, in that glorious expansionist spring of the early sixties, the new universities were being created, some of them took over and adapted the college idea, albeit in a somewhat emasculated form.   The collegiate structure made it possible to create comprehensible social communities within the larger world of the university.   The colleges of the new universities do not however have a sufficient academic base nor a shared professional purpose and in consequence they fail to become genuine colleges in the full sense of that term.   The communality they establish is that which comes from living together rather than that which comes from the sharing of an academic life and the development of a professional purpose.   The college of education has the advantage of having several communalities to hold it together - it has a shared social and residential life, a common academic purpose and a single professional aim.   In some cases there is in addition the bond of a common set of religious beliefs.   All this makes it possible for the college of education to have a powerful formative influence upon its members.   It is most unfortunate that in the debates of the last few years the advantages of this form of academic organisation have been discounted, partly, I suggest, because Lord James and some of his colleagues chose to look at its supposed disadvantages and ignored the benefits it was capable of conferring.   It is gratifying to learn that some 'monotechnics' as they are disparagingly called, are to be allowed to survive.   Too often this is being done, however, for negative reasons, because no other future seems possible.   In this paper I wish to suggest that there is a case for the monotechnic college  -  large ones as well as small ones  -  and that we owe it to those students who know from the start that they wish to teach, to keep open for them the possibility of being educated and trained in colleges entirely devoted to the task of preparing young people for the country's most important profession.   The case for getting rid of as many monotechnics as possible has not been proven.   Let us make the system of higher education fit the preparation of teachers, not vice versa.   In fairness I have to add that some of the things I have to propose will mean that there will be an even smaller survival rate for colleges.   That I accept because we must also see that the college system fits the needs of the profession and the students not vice versa.

Lord James listened to the evidence of those who opposed the monotechnic because the principles which he seized upon would not fit the monotechnic college.   He saw advantage in the postponement of choice, in consecutive rather than concurrent training and in short-cycle higher education (the Diploma of Higher Education).   I do not deny that there are students who wish to postpone their choice of career and I am glad that the system as it is developing is providing plenty of opportunity for such students many of whom will, no doubt, become excellent teachers in due course. But I also assert that there are students who know well before they take A levels - sometimes many years before - that they want to become teachers. I believe that in this group are to be found students who would welcome the full and immediate commitment to teaching which the monotechnic requires. They are likely to find attractive and self-fulfilling the very single-mindedness which opponents of the monotechnic have criticised. I will mention later some further reasons for looking again at the arguments against the monotechnic; for the moment I wish to make it clear that I am not asking for the system to return to the status quo ante bellum. I am, however, asking for a genuine mixed economy which would include monotechnics - some of them large - so that those entrants who wished to be educated and trained in a college specialising in this one important profession would have that opportunity open to them.

I urge you not to allow to pass unchallenged the criticisms - often made by those with little relevant experience - of the colleges of education. There is much to be proud of in the work of these institutions; education will be the poorer if the things in that tradition worth preserving are lost in the rough and tumble of the more broadly based foundations we are at present favouring. The colleges are not, of course, without fault but let it constantly be recalled that our primary schools at their best are a model to the world and that almost all the teachers who made those schools what they are were trained in the much-criticised colleges of education. I am seeking for ways in which the best of that tradition can be preserved and developed. Frankly I am looking for centres of specialist excellence if only to act as pace-makers and standard setters for the teacher training activities going on in the rest of the system especially in the large diversified institutions where the education of teachers will be the particular concern of a minority in a large academic board and not the prime concern of the whole institution. The majority will obviously use its voting power carefully in such a situation but nevertheless much that was once assumed will not have to be argued for and voted.

When the Prime Minister's Committee on Higher Education under

Lord Robbins reported in 1963, the colleges of education were recognised as the third partner in the family of higher education. The innovations which flowed from that excellent report - especially, of course, the B. Ed degree - brought the colleges into the family of higher education, though not in the White Paper of 1972 sense of being multi-purpose institutions. The binary policy announced in 1965 meant that there could be no place for a third force in higher education. This is plain in the text of the Woolwich speech; the question had to be fudged for a little longer but the demise of the college sector will, I suggest, be dated by historians as beginning in 1965. Significantly enough the announcement was made in a polytechnic. All was made clear in the White Paper of 1972; the colleges would not be allowed to be a separate sector and must find their future on one side or the other of the binary system. Had it not been for the awkwardness of the voluntary college position the whole re-organisation of the system might well have been carried through even more speedily. Nevertheless even for church colleges the choice is the same - jump one side or the other; you cannot stay in-between. The aim of this was not - it is fair to add - 'mere' administrative convenience. The new arrangement gave the planners that measure of flexibility in terms of regulating the supply of teachers and extending the provision of cheaper places in higher education which the system needed if it was to be adapted to the new situation developing in the late sixties. It is, of course, easy with hindsight to criticise, but my feeling is that in all these developments insufficient attention was given to the impact of the planning on the quality of teacher training. The thing made planning sense of a kind but good planning also makes educational sense and some of the arrangements we now have, or are about to develop, do not always in my view make educational sense. We must, however, be fair to the administrators since what they were proposing seemed for the most part to be in line with what the Committee headed by Lord James had recommended. A sharp-eyed observer might of course have noticed that the minority report of that Committee (despite the protestations and the euphemism that is what it is) was signed by the only experienced teacher trainers on the Committee. That minority report saw advantage in the maintenance and indeed development of the university link. The main drive of government policy has, however, had the effect of putting the colleges firmly into the further education camp; usually it is into advanced further education but it is not always so.

There may well be a case for forcing the colleges of education to come down on one side or the other of the binary divide. The terms of the usual settlement - complete assimilation by another institution - are less easily defended. Paragraph 154 of the White Paper of 1972 speaks of complete integration and when immediately after the issue of the White Paper some universities approached the UGC about mergers with local colleges, the conditions (presumably as agreed with the DES) were so severe as to make a merger very difficult indeed for any college which felt that it had something distinctive to offer. Indeed the operation seemed to be more like that of a take-over rather than a merger; there was to be one finance officer, one budget, one point of control and it seemed that the policy was to ensure that the college should lose its entire identity. My understanding is that the mergers with universities now being discussed and implemented are much less draconian though whether they will permit the evolution of what I refer to later in this paper as university colleges of education has yet to be seen.

It was rapidly realised that complete absorption was particularly difficult for Church colleges. Nevertheless the apparent easing of the arrangements has led to real progress at Exeter, Bangor and elsewhere. On the local authority side the arrangements made at Loughborough and at Warwick are a credit to all the parties concerned. I repeat my expression of hope that the universities concerned will be able to allow a genuine college-within-the-university to develop. Perhaps there is a new and important variation yet to be played on the theme of the college as a constituent of the university.

University mergers are however the exception. Most merged colleges find themselves in a polytechnic or other major college in the further education sector. Here too the principle, assumed without question from the start, seems to be that of complete absorption. The college tends to lose its separate identity; it becomes a school, faculty or even a department of the parent organisation and it has to take on the organisational pattern of the whole even when that pattern does not particularly fit the task of preparing teachers. One sometimes feels sorry for the senior staff of the receiving major institutions especially when they have had no previous experience of training teachers. The demand from the submerging college seems to be for courses providing at one and the same time a high degree of specialisation (for example, a nursery/infant teacher) within an education so broad (art, English, mathematics, environmental studies, physical education, music, religious studies, movement, drama, etc) that it seems to involve pretty well the whole of the polytechnic or college. Again I have to ask whether complete absorption is necessarily the only way of carrying through such mergers. There is a case, especially (and this is an important proviso) when the DES can be persuaded to keep a substantial number of teacher training places in the institution, for the polytechnic or other large college to consider the possibility of administrative arrangements which fall short of submersion. Too often, but understandably enough since this follows the logic of paragraph 154, the question has been phrased as 'How can the college be fitted into the polytechnic structure?' when it would have been better to have asked, 'Can the polytechnic modify its structure so as to accommodate this highly specialised (and admittedly rather peculiar) college?'. I am not suggesting that this is necessarily the best approach in all cases; I am prepared to guess that in most cases bearing in mind that teacher training numbers will be small and that the college will have been merged into the larger unit to facilitate diversification, much the best solution is for the college to be fully integrated and to become a department or at best a school of the larger institution. But there may well be some cases - a few but significant - where numbers permit and local needs dictate a different arrangement. To develop this point I need now to carry out another small excursion into the history of higher education to elucidate another use of the term 'college' in an academic context. I wish to call to your mind the case of the university colleges of between the wars.

There are today many great universities, some with significant international reputations, which began their academic life as university colleges under the tutelage - as Lord James would put it - of another academic institution. In the story of the expansion of higher education in this century, the new universities receive most notice but it is the former university colleges which made the most substantial contribution. The university college tradition has been allowed to lapse; perhaps it is time for it to be revived.

You will have guessed that I have at last got to the main point of this article. I wish to suggest that we should husband sufficient training places to establish a handful of substantial university or polytechnic colleges of education entirely devoted - in the initial stages at any rate - to the training and education of teachers. The relationship with the parent body, be it a polytechnic or a university, would be symbiotic; though there would be a measure of independence the one could not exist without the other The polytechnic or university college would be able to develop the life-style it judged to be suitable for the professional purpose of the college. The organisational structures would reflect the same specialist outcome; the academic board would be entirely devoted to this and would have the right to treat directly with validating bodies and eventually to award its own degrees. The teaching profession would be strongly represented in the councils of the college. Such a college could rapidly become the brightest star in the crown of the polytechnic or university to which it was attached.

If one goes along with this idea at all it is important to realise what the price would be. After all the figures in the DES Report on Education No 82 of March 1975 remain no matter how we organise things and 500 more places here must mean 500 less somewhere else. I see these few monotechnics - mainly large - as providing the core of teacher supply with guaranteed numbers and a steady output. Adjustments year by year to cope with fluctuations in demand would be made in the places better placed to adjust - that is in diversified colleges, in polytechnic departments and in university departments of education. Above all I see the university or polytechnic colleges of education as centres not only of high activity but of excellence, setting the standards by which the rest are to be judged, preserving and developing the tradition to which I referred earlier in this article and establishing themselves as major centres for research in pedagogy. It follows that the staff appointed to these colleges would be recruited nationally and internationally; they would not get a post in the establishment by virtue of being in the institution when it was designated. Validation could come from either side of the binary system though in due course they might well become chartered bodies able to validate themselves. Surely teaching is important enough to have like business management its centres of high activity and - hopefully - excellence. Perhaps we shall in due course be able to welcome to the community of higher education the University College of Education, Coventry, the Polytechnic College of Education, Falmer, and other major centres, where all that is best in teacher education and training is to be found, taught and developed.

We must not, however, be unrealistic and I must refer again to the figures in DES Report No 82. If anything, these projections are optimistic for they are using the government's 1974 demographic forecast which assumes an upturn in the birth rate because of the guess that couples are postponing rather than refusing to have children. We now know that in the early months of 1975 the rate has continued to decline. We should therefore continue to regard the figure of 12,000 new entrants each year to three and four year courses as firm and one to be achieved long before this decade is out. Even lower figures might become necessary. How many of these precious places can we afford to give designated centres of high activity? The more places they have the less there will be for other institutions. On the other hand it would be reasonable to forbid such centres from diversifying in any way and this would leave that field clearer for other institutions. Indeed, there is much to be said for concentrating diversified courses (new liberal arts courses, for example) in fewer institutions and there is a special case for concentrating them in colleges absorbed into polytechnics and other large colleges, free-standing or otherwise. It is particularly distressing for a validating body such as the CNAA to find that in doing its best for a college trying to develop courses other than those leading to a teaching qualification, it is cutting the supply of students to a similar course it has already validated elsewhere. Universities in their validating role feel this pressure less strongly for they are usually helping colleges validated by them to develop courses different from those offered in the university. The present policy of share-the-cuts-all-round has resulted in a proliferation of diversified courses being offered at a time when the number of qualified applicants for such degree courses is stationary. We have scarcely viable penny-packet B. Ed courses in far too many places and now we are developing hopelessly uneconomic halfpenny BA packets in even more places. It is for these reasons that I would prevent the centres of high activity in teacher training from entering the BA field. This is not to say that those places which had to drop out of the initial training operation would be kept out of all contact with teaching; the in-service side would certainly have to continue for though initial training may conveniently be concentrated in rather fewer places than we have had hitherto, the need in in-service training is for centres within travelling distance of every teacher in the country. These are considerations to be kept in mind as Mr Prentice begins the final stage of his plan for the final pruning of the teacher training system. My own view is that the system should be reduced even more than the amount suggested in the Secretary of State's reply in the Commons on 20th March last. The 60,000 places outside universities will consist of up to 7,500 post-graduates, some 12,000 to 13,000 in-service places - that is perhaps 20,000 full time equivalent over and above those taking initial courses which would total some 40,000. The in-service places as I have already suggested can and should be provided in a large number of institutions, for the convenience of the teacher and to make day-release possible. It would be wrong to concentrate in-service places in a few institutions apart from specialist places provided on a national basis. The polytechnics will undoubtedly press for a large share of the post-graduate places to be allocated to their education departments. We must then think of concentrating the three and four year initial training places in even fewer institutions. We must always remember that some of those places will be specialist places (home economics and physical education, for example) not capable of being allocated to the usual run of colleges. It is probable then that we will end up with a number of closures greater than the Secretary of State's figure of 30. I see the initial training places as being distributed firstly amongst a few university or polytechnic colleges of education, secondly a few specialist colleges, thirdly a very small number of small colleges justified by reference to the particular circumstances of their position, fourthly a few free-standing colleges of higher education with education departments situated in areas not served by polytechnics, and finally education departments in polytechnics. There will still, of course, be some 5,000 training places for graduates in universities and these should be maintained for teaching must maintain a presence on either side of the binary line. The UGC should have (and no doubt has) ensured that no more university training departments are opened, unless it be as a result of a merger with a college of education.

I now wish in the final part of my paper to turn to the 'university' part of the title. I claim that the university record in relation to the colleges of education has, taken as a whole, been one of which the universities may be proud. One of the more hurtful blows delivered by Lord James was to characterise the misdeeds of a few universities as the general view of all. Quite remarkable progress was made in a relatively short time; though Lord Robbins did not report until late in 1963, by 1968 five universities had already graduated their first B. Ed students. By 1974, 23 universities were doing likewise and well over 5,000 B. Ed degrees were awarded in that year. Then, with a remarkable flexibility, which gives the lie to the critics, no less than 17 universities have developed in-service B. Ed degrees In 1974 my university alone graduated 158 serving teachers as Bachelors of Education and of these no less than 73%

obtained a second class degree or better. But I do not wish to make the same mistake as Lord James - generalising from the atypical. Some universities have not risen as readily or as enthusiastically to the opportunity provided by the suggestions in the Robbins report in relation to the work of the colleges of education. Fortunately the Robbins report also contained another provision from which the CNAA has emerged. It is sad that some great universities formerly active in the world of teacher training have seen the existence of the CNAA as a justification for breaking their links with the colleges but that is what autonomy is all about. It includes the right to be negative as well as creative. Those universities which have remained interested as validating bodies are adding to the great variety of courses now available. The CNAA deserves credit for adding significantly to the store of ideas about course construction and for ensuring that the experience of work with the CNAA is available to those who work on the university side of the line as well as to those who are in the public sector.

University validation differs from the CNAA validation. Though universities are national and international institutions, in their work as validating bodies they operate as local organisations. This is at once their strength and their weakness as validating bodies. Because they rely on local and continuing contact with known people whom they meet regularly in a professional capacity and sometimes as friends, because they know that if the known person leaves they will be consulted about the replacement, university assessors can and do take what the CNAA might regard as risks. This shows particularly in the present exercise where units have been reduced in size to the point at which individual subject teams are often only marginally viable. The university knows that as a last resort (and such things have been done) the course can be sustained by providing extra teaching from the university or indeed by bringing the student to the university when a suitable course is available. Such particular and emergency arrangements can be made without fuss on a local basis; the CNAA would no doubt act similarly in an emergency but - for sound and understandable reasons - it needs to be assured before the course starts that such an occurrence would be most unlikely to occur. The particularity of university validation can also however be a drawback as those who have their curricular wishes unduly influenced by a prevailing view in the university department most nearly concerned will know though even the CNAA has to rely on judgements (which some might call the prejudices) of particular individuals. On the resources side there is, of course, the fact that in most cases the university library is available to provide the support which lecturers need to sustain their teaching at an appropriate level. In my view it would now be reasonable for the polytechnic libraries to provide a similar service to all CNAA colleges in their area. Every institution providing degree courses should provide the library backing needed by the students; the cost of research libraries for the use of staff is today such that it would be irresponsible for us not to regionalise such facilities.

The breaking up of the world of teacher education as we have known it is in many ways a matter for regret. I can be brief here because the paper by Norman Evans puts the problem extremely well. He points out that there are values, skills and awarenesses which we must preserve whatever the system we are to work under. Teacher educators have a key position in the world of education; whatever the structural changes, however much we be dispersed into institutions with other purposes and remustered into unions with a different centre of gravity, we must ensure that our particular community of scholars with its unique relationship with the profession, the education service, the government, the local authorities and the wider world of higher education, remains as an identifiable group able to speak out as a group when necessary and continues to be dedicated to the preservation and extension of that fine tradition of teacher training of which we are the inheritors. We owe it to the children in the schools to preserve our corporate identity. However we teacher educators be dispersed, merged, taken-over, re-deployed, diversified or even wound up, we have a unique contribution to make to the nation's thinking about education; we need not only conferences but a standing body (preferably not one involved in union affairs) to provide the system with the wisdom passed on to us and the fruit of our experience as the shapers of those who in turn will shape the children who are our future.

# The Changing Curriculum

After the rapid growth of the 1960s a period of calm evaluation was needed, a time to pick up the lost opportunities. There can be few colleges that have enjoyed the luxury of a period long enough to plan, run and develop a course without urgent new course planning disturbing the process. The vast growth in students was matched by the growth of staff, and these lecturers had no sooner entered college than they were asked to design B. Ed degrees, part-time B. Eds, three-year B. Ed degrees and now, diversified BAs. Change has become the norm and perhaps some valuable aspects of curriculum development overlooked. Time for thoughtful and insightful discussion of conceptual frameworks for the new courses has been missing and the result has often been that planning has occasionally been rather 'hit or miss' and possibly lacking in rigour.

Edwin Kerr initiates this section by detailing the CNAA's role in validation processes. He describes perceptively the principles and practice of validation in a paper which clearly identifies some of the pitfalls of curriculum construction. He stresses the Council's flexibility in handling curriculum proposals and its insistence on maintaining a responsible attitude to academic standards. By 'thinking aloud' in this way he hopes that he has helped others to avoid submitting ill-prepared courses for validation and that he has encouraged colleges to construct courses from their obvious real strengths and resources.

Anthony Becher, lately Assistant Director at the Nuffield Foundation and member of the Nuffield Higher Education Group, proposes that it is only by sharing curriculum concerns that teachers in higher education will be able to break through the binary line. He underlines the importance of curriculum change to teacher education rather than the institutional and structural changes which appear to take the headlines. By describing various models for curriculum development and relating curricular innovation elsewhere to teacher education he suggests that individual colleges do not have to 'discover the wheel' for themselves. He stresses that colleges now have an opportunity, despite the many constraints, to design and develop coherent and stimulating new courses.

Kenneth Gardner in his discussion on modularity attempts both to define the difference between modular and linear courses with a simple criterion and to demonstrate that modularity in a modified form has much to offer. How far we need to balance our compromises in the practice of curriculum construction needs to be judged finely but his article does help to suggest some of the factors in the equation.

# Principles and practice of validation

Edwin Kerr

I want to look at the area which, in theory, was to be at the interface between the two parts of this series of articles. The first part of the book has concentrated on the re-organisational factors. The book is now moving on to deal with curriculum factors, and this contribution is meant to be the change-over point between them. At the outset, however, it might be useful to say a word or two in historical retrospect on the way the CNAA developed. The CNAA was proposed in the Robbins Report of 1963. The proposal was accepted immediately by the Government, and the Charter was granted to the Council in 1964. Of course there was a preceding body but it was only concerned with the validation of awards in science and technology. It is interesting now in historical retrospect to look at the Robbins recommendations on CNAA because they were on the bases that as institutions developed and reached a certain degree of experience and standing under the CNAA, they might then move over into the university sector. I believe the Robbins Committee always looked on CNAA as a sort of midwife that would develop institutions up to a certain stage, bring them to birth as universities, whilst it would itself always stay a relatively small organisation, never to become large or influential. It has been said that the Open University is the biggest university in the country in terms of student numbers, but the biggest degree awarding body in terms of student numbers is now the CNAA. There are at present over sixty thousand students registered on first degrees of the Council. Ten years ago that would have been unthinkable.

To turn to the theme of validation itself and the way the Council has operated. I think it may be of some value if I describe the process fairly briefly and succinctly, possibly revealing some of the attitudes of the Council more than talking about the details of the process. I want to look first of all in general terms before moving to the particular terms of its role in the validation of teacher education courses.

I think there is possibly one thing I should point out at the very start and that is that the Council's role is an academic one, purely and entirely. We exist to validate courses, make academic judgements on the viability of courses and the associated resources. We do not have a planning role, nor do we have any role in the questions of higher education supply, nor in the actual location of courses. As you know, these things are done by the machinery of the Regional Advisory Council and the DES, so that we only get courses after judgements have been made that they are necessary on the grounds of need and the availability of resources. That's the theoretical position - it is also the actual position, though there is an increasing volume of interest in the Council that the position is not always logical, for we are frequently asked to validate courses when it is not apparent that there is a need for an additional course in that subject area or that the proposed location for the course is the best one. And so one of the themes that is of increasing interest to the Council is, how can the questions of the co-ordination of higher education, the planning of it and the location of the courses, be decided in the public sector in such a way that the decisions are firmly based on real academic knowledge of the system and not based too much on horse-trading and political judgement? That's not part of my brief at the moment, but it is none-the-less a very interesting thing for the future.

The Council has a Royal Charter which details its responsibilities. The fundamental object of the Council is specified in Article 2 of the Charter and although this is in the stilted language of a legal document, I should nevertheless like to reproduce it, because it does throw light upon the powers and responsibilities of the Council very clearly: 'The object of the Council shall be the advancement of education, learning and knowledge by means of the grant of academic awards and distinctions and for the purpose of promoting that object it shall determine the conditions governing the award of such distinctions and approve courses of study to be pursued by candidates to qualify for such awards'. Picking out two or three of the phrases in that and emphasising them, the Council is empowered to act in the whole of the United Kingdom. Its power is the power to grant academic awards and distinctions, which is largely in the granting of degrees, but there are other academic awards as well. The Council is empowered to determine the conditions to be associated with its awards, and it might be thought that as we have now something like eight hundred degree courses approved we should have a massive set of regulations and conditions. I would claim that although it does take several pages to write down the regulations and the framework associated with our degrees, that none-the-less those regulations are characterised by considerable flexibility. In fact, I think they are now considerably more flexible than they were three or fours years ago, but with the increased flexibility of the regulations it has called for more responsibility on the part of the proposing institutions. We are now virtually saying in our regulations, that within the framework you will have to choose what you want to do, that you will have to choose a consistent sub-set of these regulations and justify that the sub-set then meets the requirements of the course you are proposing, and, indeed, that the regulations that you are suggesting from among this set fit the course. Thus I think I could sustain my claim that the regulations are very flexible and that they are no bar on innovation or new course structures and design. The next fundamental article I want to pick out from the Charter is the power to approve particular courses of study. Now, in itself that is a very interesting thing. It identifies the debate which did go on to some extent, not very publicly at the time, and is still going on, and that is, should the Council's power be a responsibility to approve individual courses, or should it be a power to approve institutions, and then, having approved the institutions, to allow the institutions to design their own courses? At the moment, the power is very clearly the responsibility to approve particular courses.

This is all I really wanted to say on the general position and now I want to turn to how the Council operates its procedures of validation. I want first of all to do this in general terms and then move on to the particular situation in education. The Council's procedures have evolved over the past sixteen years or so, and although the Council itself has only been in existence for a little over ten years, when it was established it did take over the procedures of the preceding Council. Nevertheless during that time, the procedures have evolved considerably and are still evolving; therefore the present procedures in use I would by no means describe as the definitive set. For example, Alec Ross has used the phrase that the Council might develop an agency situation in which colleges could do some of the work internally for and on behalf of the Council. This is something which is being explored within the Council at the moment, and it is the hope that a discussion paper on an extension of the validation procedures will be issued by the Council to all interested parties, probably before this summer. So the present procedures are still evolving and, I think, will continue to evolve. A phrase that I often use at conferences and meetings with staff, which describes the sort of situation that I would like to see developing, and which I think to a large extent has developed, is a situation of partnership. I do not believe that it is the CNAA on one side and the colleges on the other and that it is a 'them-and-us' situation because frequently colleges have members of staff proposing a course one day and the next one of them is a member of a CNAA visiting party doing exactly the same sort of exercise in some other college. It is a combined effort, a relationship of partnership between the Council and the associated colleges.

To understand the situation in detail, it is probably necessary to describe, very briefly, the internal organisation so that this can be seen in its perspective. To do this I would say that there are essentially three levels within the Council. There is the Council itself which, if you describe this in institutional terms, is virtually an amalgamation between the governing body of a college and the academic board in that the Council is charged with matters of finance and property, staffing, and legal concerns. It is also charged with making the final academic decisions of the CNAA. Underneath that it has got four or five main committees which are really like faculty boards, boards of school, call them what you will. These cover broad areas of work, such as arts and social studies, art and design, sciences and technology and, the one that we are particularly interested in in this context, education. Then, underneath most of these committees, there are individual subject boards which look at courses. Thus, for example, under the committee for arts and social studies there is a sociological studies board, a humanities board, etc. Under the committee for education the situation is rather different and I will describe the reasons why and the ways in which it is different later. Thus the Council makes the regulations that determine the overall framework, the committees, if you liken them to faculty boards, review the operation of the subject boards and ensure that there is consistency of practice, and when changes in regulations are needed, they advise the Council on these changes. The subject boards themselves are the validating instruments, and they are the grass-roots level where the really heavy work of the Council is carried out.

The membership of these bodies is again fairly easy to describe. The Council of the CNAA itself is about thirty people, roughly one-third university, one-third college and the remaining third being local authority and industry. The committees are each roughly thirty to forty strong, and there is the same tri-partite make-up on them but the boards vary in size, depending on the work-load. The total membership, and this is really a tribute to the interest of people in curriculum development and validation drawn from the universities and colleges, is now somewhere over a thousand. This is a tremendous tribute to the extent of voluntary work that people are prepared to put in on this; obviously expenses are paid but no fees. Sometimes the Council has been charged with being over-dominated by universities and those who have an interest to protect the status quo. I always refute this charge in two ways. First, I point out that the Council could not have operated without the university involvement, for we owe a tremendous debt of gratitude to those from the universities who have participated in the boards. I think many of them would say in their turn that they have gained by operating in the Council's boards. Secondly, that the university members have proved very willing to approve innovations and new curricular experiments. I might add that fifty per cent or rather more, of the total membership is drawn from the associated institutions. In that sense, once an institution is validated it joins the club and assists in the validation of other institutions.

Now, the Council has said that in its procedures for validation, it will look essentially at three things, and it has placed these in order of priority. It will look first at the college as a totality, then it would look at the staff who are to be associated with the course, and finally it would look at the documents describing the proposed course and its curriculum, and so on. I think that arguably the first two could be put on a par, they might even be interchanged, the college and the staff, but I certainly say that both those are more important than the documents.

What then do we mean by looking at the college itself? By this we mean looking at the way the college functions, the nature of its work, the way it manages itself, and how it makes its academic decisions. Thus we consider its academic board to ascertain whether it really deals with academic questions, or merely concentrates on administrative matters which are of secondary importance. Has the academic board got a structure beneath it that matches the courses that it wants to offer? That is, we discuss the organisation of their faculties, or departments, or schools, and see whether these match the types of courses that they are putting up. And, really above all, we look at the college as a community, to see if it hangs together, if it encourages research, and how it is planning for the future. This sort of investigation is usually done in a separate visit, concentrating on these aspects alone. We usually do this once every five years.

If we turn now to the consideration of a particular course proposal, as I have said the second thing we look at is the staff and that arguably this might be put first. The type of thing we are looking at here are the levels of leadership that will be provided for the course as a whole and the important main components of it. We are really trying to form a judgement on the academic vitality of the staff. Are they seriously thinking on curriculum matters? Are they up to date? Are they engaged in research or consultancy or the development of new teaching methods? My justification for putting that ahead of the actual documents describing a course would simply be that if the staff are of good, high quality you can always put a course right. If they are not, then you might as well go away and tell them you are not going to validate the course. It is as stark as that!

This is really the answer to the question implied in Norman Mackenzie's introductory article. Courses in physics aren't the same as courses in sociology. In reality, what we are doing when we are validating is forming academic judgements on the suitability of the staff to teach degree courses. I then get charged, or the Council gets charged, with the impossibility of doing that task within a day, or a day and a half as the case may be. To which I retort, we appoint our members of staff on half-hour to an hour interviews and by and large don't make many mistakes.

This is where the documents come in. A person seeking an appointment writes his curriculum vitae which gives you something to talk about and form judgements about his suitability for appointment to an institution. So, in exactly the same way, the documents describing a course are, in the Council's view, the statement from the proposing institution, and in particular from the proposing staff, of what they think they can do, and how they would work together as a team to teach this particular course. We judge them on their own claims, and I think this is a procedure which can be defended. I am very interested in Alec Ross saying that this procedure is now beginning to wear off on to some universities, who are in effect saying that we ought to put on a course in this area, but we want to make sure that this has been thoroughly thought through and that those who are going to teach it know why they chose certain ways to do it rather than other possible solutions. That is exactly the essence of what has come to be described as the CNAA procedure. Getting those who are going to teach the course in front of their academic peers, having a discussion and seeing that they really have thought through the essence of what they want to teach. I would emphasise again that the Council doesn't have any standard prescribed mode for courses. The Council doesn't think that there are certain types of courses that can only be operated in polytechnics and other sorts of courses that can only be offered in universities. The Council probably does believe that if you draw a spectrum of the courses, those that operate under the Council's aegis have probably got a mean point which is closer to the applied end, the vocational end than is true if you drew a similar spectrum of university courses.

Before turning to the situation in education, perhaps it is worth making one additional point about validation. I have been talking about the colleges offering the courses and the courses themselves and the way validation procedure works in general terms. I think I should say that right throughout its existence, the Council has been working with institutions that have their courses validated by more than one body. For example, we have been used to working with many polytechnics and other institutions, part of whose work is validated by the CNAA, and, in the past, part of which has been validated by the University of London. Again other parts of them are validated by professional institutions. So the Council is used to this system which is now, in jargon, described as a mixed-economy situation. It may cause difficulty inside a college to work with a multiplicity of validating bodies, but it doesn't cause a major theological difficulty to the Council. We are quite prepared to work with institutions that work with more than one validating body. This is particularly relevant in this situation in Brighton where the degree work in the present Polytechnic is validated by the Council. If the new Polytechnic, with the College of Education as part of it, decides that the work in teacher education should be validated by the University of Sussex, this will not worry the Council at all. The Council is perfectly prepared to work in that situation. I think that there are some problems that will arise that will need discussion and exploration to work out solutions. For example, suppose the University validates the B. Ed in the College and the Council validates the BAs down the road in the present Polytechnic, and there is a Dip. H. E. situation in it with the possibility of transfer of students back and forward in either direction. Obviously the College, the University, the Polytechnic and the Council will have to sit down and work out how to cope with that sort of situation. But, as I hope to give an example a little later on which isn't public knowledge yet, I think we have succeeded in doing just that in one particular case of a college/CNAA/university involvement and I think with good will these other issues can be dealt with as and when they do arise.

Now, turning to the education situation itself. If a meeting on teacher education had been held four years ago, the Council would not have been invited to attend, even though the Council has had a Committee for Education since 1967. In its early days it was only moderately busy, and for various reasons it did not validate any courses. One or two were proposed to it in the late sixties but were not validated, partly because the Council had not requested the DES to designate it as a relevant organisation within the teacher regulations, and the relationships therefore with ATOs had not been properly sorted out. This was delayed until the early seventies. At that stage, it became evident that things were going to change, that the Council was going to be involved with teacher education on a large scale, and the Council itself recognised that it would therefore have to expand its Committee for Education and to work out a whole range of procedures and academic questions. They guessed, even at that stage, that approximately a third to a half of the colleges and students involved in teacher education would eventually be associated with the Council and so there would be major new challenges thrown up for the Council to solve. Now, some of these challenges we have had to deal with in a short space of time over the last three years or so include, for example, the preparation of academic guidelines for the Diploma of Higher Education, for the B. Ed, for the Postgraduate Certificate of Education, and for the in-service B. Ed and there are still a range of other things that have to be worked out; some of which I may refer to at the end of my paper. We here had to recruit senior staff for the Council who were knowledgeable about the situation in education, who could give the leadership to our various committees and boards on the education side, and we had to reconstitute the Council's Committee itself so that it would indeed be able to do the increased amount of work that would come to it. The Committee for Education is now somewhat different from the other committees in that it is roughly composed in the following way: various members of the Council itself appointed from the Council, members appointed from the local authority associations, members appointed from colleges with approved courses, members from the teachers' professional associations and members appointed from the higher education bodies concerned with teacher education, such as ATCDE, UTEC, etc About a quarter of the Committee itself is drawn from the group of professional associations for teachers, because we felt that if there were going to be professional degrees, we must have a high representation from the teachers' professional associations.

The other main thing that we had to do during this preparatory stage, and what is still going on, is a vast amount of advisory work to the colleges. My colleagues spend a lot of their time going to colleges, meeting the staff, talking to them about their proposals, answering questions on the Council's procedures and so on. A great deal has been done within the last three years. A lot still remains to be done. But certainly the staff of the Council who have been on the education side have borne the 'brunt of the battle' in a very remarkable way. The B. Ed guidelines themselves - which I don't want to talk about in detail but this was a very interesting exercise - arise from the 1972 White Paper. In spite of the remarks about the White Paper, that it should have been called a framework for contraction, I still believe it was correctly titled, because if you compare the situation in 1972 and the probable figure now of 600, 000 or thereabouts, it still constitutes an expansion on the 1972 situation. Perhaps it is not quite as rapid an expansion to three-quarters of a million as was stated in the White Paper, or the million that some people wanted, but it still is expansion. There may be, indeed there is, contraction in one part of the system that we have been talking about, but overall it is still expansion.

As soon as that White Paper became public knowledge, it became apparent that the Dip. H. E. and the new B. Ed and the rundown in the Certificate in Education were going to affect both sides of our planning and it did seem to Sir Kenneth Berrill, the then Chairman of the University Grants Committee, and myself that it would be illogical to allow the two parts of binary to go off in their own separate ways without any transbinary talks, and so, as is now public knowledge, we did have the two study groups, one of which set up guidelines on the Dip. H. E. and the other guidelines on the B. Ed. The CNAA adopted both sets of guidelines as its interim ones. As we have been validating a few Dip. H. E. s and we have got a number more under consideration, I would guess that in a few months, in the light of our experience, we will want to modify the guidelines here and there. The B. Ed guidelines, I think, are still satisfactory though it is probable, again in due course, that in the light of experience one would want to reflect on them and possibly modify them a bit. The important aspect as far as I am concerned is the emphasis in the early parts of the guidelines that there was here a new situation with B. Eds designed as degrees right from the stage when the students entered the college rather than having to come through the Certificate and going on to the B. Ed from the Certificate. This was a new situation, which required fresh consideration, and that solutions should not be closely prescribed, for there should be the need for experiments and yet that some structure and some coherence must be apparent in each course proposal. There are in paragraphs 20 - 24 points that have to be faced up to in the design of each course. For example, where is the degree challenge, the place of study of education and philosophy in the proposed course, the place of academic study (if there is to be an academic study), the role of the periods of school placement, the ways in which the exercise of skills can be developed? All these are questions which a CNAA validating party would want to discuss with the proposers of the course to see their particular solutions to the problem. Let me stress again that we would have expected the proposers to have worked out their own solutions and to be able to defend them.

I was a little bit surprised on reading in one of the discussion papers and perhaps I read it too hurriedly and didn't quite get the drift of it, but it did seem to me that one of the discussion papers was suggesting that it was compulsory to have a Dip. H. E. within a B. Ed.  As far as the Council is concerned, and as far as the B. Ed guidelines are concerned, such a situation is not compulsory.  There is no obligation to have a Dip. H. E. within a B. Ed and therefore one doesn't need to be in a situation where a Dip. H. E. might be distorting a B. Ed.   It can be in it, but there is no forced inclusion of it as far as the Council is concerned. The Council does regard the B. Ed as a course which is concerned with the professional preparation of future teachers, a course in which all parts including the professional and curriculum parts are treated very seriously.   I think it is fair to say that the Council does not regard the B. Ed as a joint honours course, a course in which on the one hand you have the study of education and on the other hand an academic subject. It regards it as an integrated study, and this is a not unimportant point when one comes to discuss the questions of validation of BA course composed of the same modules that were put in B. Ed courses, but I'll say a bit more about that a little later on.

A word, then, about the validation of the B. Ed courses, which in one or two ways is different from the general pattern.  I described earlier the position of the main committees of the Council underneath which there were other specialist subject boards, and I gave one or two examples. You could multiply those examples through mathematics, physics, chemistry, etc.   Those are situations which are quite simple where you get courses in individual discipline areas, where it is pretty easy to say which is the correct board to put it to.  The situation in education isn't like that.  The courses don't split up into nice separate components; and so we have not got underneath the committee for education a range of subject boards to which particular courses are referred.  The Committee for Education does its own validation.  But of course it is ludicrous to think of forty people validating the amount of work we have been doing on education, and so we have got a considerable number of people who support the committee in panels. You have got an educational panel, a science panel, arts and craft panel, and so on. These panels are called upon to augment a core group from the Committee for Education itself. So, when we are dealing with a proposal from a college, a small group from the Committee is selected and it is supported by various members drawn from the other panels. The core group is not normally more than ten drawn from the Committee for Education, sometimes less than that and this may be supported by quite a large number of people from the panels, depending on the complexity and range of the course that is being considered. Indeed, on occasions, the total visiting party may build up to about forty people because some of the courses may have fifteen options in them, and as we like to take at least two people per option, that soon builds up. The validation of education courses really takes place in two stages to which on occasions may be added the preceding informal consultations between the Council's own staff and the proposers. In the first stage, the core group from the Committee for Education meet the college to talk about the structure of the course, college facilities, the way the course is planned, the way it is proposed to lead it, and the role of professional and educational studies in the course. This usually takes a day in itself. It isn't usually a day spent in a room like this, but at some stage we break up and go round the college to see the facilities and talk to the staff in their own environment. In the second stage the various areas of study are looked at in detail, and again I would emphasise that what we are doing is talking to the staff and assessing their suitability to teach the course that they have proposed. Sometimes these two stages are done on consecutive days, so there is a two-day visit to the institution, but sometimes they are separated by a period of time.

Now I have already stressed the great importance that we attach to the objectives of the course. I just want to say that we will certainly have expected that the proposers will have worked out their own objectives for the overall course and that they will also have worked out objectives for the components within that course. We certainly want to test the components and the objectives for the components against the objectives for the overall course. Let me give an example of what I mean. If it had been stated that here is a course in which there are academic subjects, and the academic subjects are planned in integration with the professional studies, then it is a fair question for the Council to ask that it be demonstrated how this planning was actually done, and where the professional studies reinforce the academic studies and vice versa We asked that one question in one particular college and we were told 'Ah, this particular academic subject was planned in total isolation from the professional studies!', even though the stated objectives of the course was integration. Not surprisingly, the course as submitted was not approved. It was referred back so that the planning could match its own stated objectives. That is one example of the way in which the Council uses this philosophy of looking at objectives.

Now staff is another important area I have stressed. Quite often the Council does say 'Yes, we like the design of the course, we like the overall structure, we like the particular structure, but you haven't got enough staff to teach certain parts of it. You will need to get them', (and we will specify the types of additional or different staff needed). In the past, when we were still in a fairly rapid state of expansion, that didn't usually provide any problem to a college - they were able to recruit the additional staff. Now it does provide a very different situation. We say to a college that they need to get additional psychologists or sociologists, but they may not be in a situation where they can get new staff, or they may be in a situation where they are trying to reduce their total staff. The question is then often asked, what is the Council going to do about this? The answer is - the Council's not going to do anything about it! The Council's not going to change its academic judgements, it cannot, it has got the chartered responsibility to make these academic judgements and if it makes an academic judgement of that sort and the proposing college cannot fulfil that judgement, then in the Council's opinion that course cannot start until that particular condition has been fulfilled. This is possibly a difficult thing to say and yet I think it is the only realistic thing for the Council to say unless it is going to lower standards and I don't think the Council is in business to lower standards. It is charged with the responsibility of ensuring that its degrees are comparable to the degrees of the universities of the United Kingdom and although we all know that such degrees are not equal, I don't think that the Council is setting out to validate at the lowest possible level. We are aiming to validate above the minimum.

Now, one of the other points I want to stress is that in the Council's opinion the involvement of serving teachers in the whole process is very important. We ask colleges to indicate how they have involved teachers in the planning process, by that I mean more than actually discussing with them the organisation of teaching practice; rather, how they really involve them in the planning process. We have got teachers on the Council's own Committee and in the groups that go to validate. We believe that the team of external examiners for a course should contain one or more experienced serving teachers. And so there are a number of ways in which we are trying to make our contribution to closing the gap between the schools and the colleges or increasing the partnership between the two.

We have the normal practice in most courses, if we approve them, of approving them for a period of five years, during which the college can run the course, make its own decisions, change the emphases within the course etc. But in the B. Ed courses we are faced with the special situation that course numbers are running down and that the courses we approved in 1974 and 1975 will not be running in the same way in 1979 and 1980. And so we have had to institute a system of annual monitoring so that we can look at the viability of the courses as the run-down in entry numbers begins to bite. In many ways this is regrettable, it is not something that we like to do and yet it seems that there is no other way in which it seems that we can cope with this particular problem. The Council is very concerned about viability, and its way of dealing with the situation is this one of annual monitoring.

I have been trying to paint a picture of flexibility and I think possibly one of the best ways of demonstrating flexibility is to give one or two particular examples of the things that have been validated. I don't want to go into a great deal of detail, but what I do want to say is that we are prepared to accept quite different patterns as solutions to the same problems, provided they have been properly thought through by the staff, and that the staff have got the resources and facilities to carry through their own proposals. In fact, one might think that as we have got one plus two, and two plus two, and two plus one structures that the situation is fairly chaotic. I would say as a national validating body we must be prepared to look at quite different patterns, provided we insist on quality and I think we are certainly endeavouring to insist uniformly on the quality, and that we will not accept a solution if in our opinion it will not lead to a high quality of education for the students following that course. The Times Educational Supplement, in an editorial on 14th March 1975, said the CNAA must see that professional teacher training does not get diluted either in an hors d'oeuvres course of units and modules or in striving for the conventional academic respectability. I think we are well aware of both these dangers and I think we have steered clear of both of them. That's probably a fairly tall claim to make and yet again, I think its truth could be demonstrated.

Let me just, therefore, give one or two examples of things that we have approved. We have approved quite a number of courses that are organised on a modular or unit basis, frequently these have been organised in such a way that there is a compulsory core within the courses so that fragmentation is prevented. I don't think we have approved a single course based on what could be called a cafeteria system. One of the courses we have approved is based on what could be called a one plus two structure in which the higher education base is laid in the first year and then in the second and third years an increasing proportion of the time is allocated to compulsory professional studies. Another course is exactly the converse of that; it is organised on a two plus one structure. In the first two years between a third and a half, depending on the student choice, is allocated to educational theory, followed by a professional year. So you can see the two converse examples of that sort. Then in one or two cases, which are particularly relevant to the primary and middle school and are quite innovative, there is no conventional main subject in them at all. Some of the discussion papers wonder how much innovation has gone on. I think in a number of colleges that have come to the Council there is quite a lot of this, demonstrating for example a total professional orientation within some of the course. Other courses have got a very heavy concentration of professional preparation of the teacher and an analysis of the role that the teacher actually plays in the classroom. At the minute we have one example which is quite unique in that it is virtually adding on education to an approved modular course leading to a BA degree. This is the first example we have had of this sort, in that we have added on to the BA a B. Ed in such a way that the educational studies in the B. Ed also can become a part of the BA, and the approved parts of the BA can become academic studies in the B. Ed. This is between a college and a polytechnic that had the BA approved and this seems to be in some cases a very fruitful way of moving, rather than trying to design a B. Ed and then adding, or trying to add on, a BA within the same particular college.

One of the examples I did want to mention which is just about to be approved, is a co-operation, in the transbinary sense, between a college of education which is running an approved CNAA course and a university. The course will run on the following basis: the first two years will be in the university following science education, the third year will be in the college which will be the professional year, and the fourth year will be back in the university following science education. At the end of these four years the successful graduate will get a BSc with honours in science education from the university, and a Certificate in Education from the Council. In practice it doesn't actually divide into a two plus one plus one arrangement as I have just described, as it is really closer to a two plus two structure because the Council, the university and the college have discussed this together and felt that the third year was bound to influence the fourth year and the fourth year to influence the third year. So although the third year is mainly CNAA college, there is university involvement in it and although the fourth year is mainly university, conversely there is some CNAA involvement. Nevertheless the third and fourth years do fit together. Both the Council and the university validating bodies have been involved jointly in approving this and they will also be jointly involved in approving the external examiners. So this is an interesting development. There is one similar case being discussed at the moment between the Council and the Open University. I could go on expanding examples of what is being validated but I think I have really given enough examples to justify my contention that the Council is willing to be flexible on these matters.

I want to look at the relationships with the Certificate in Education, as I know it is a subject of interest. In the Council we were certainly anxious to ensure that degree standards were set at an unambiguously high level and that they were not compromised in any way by lower standards which might be appropriate for a Certificate. So we have been prepared to look at one or two different ways of coping with this problem in the main. There is method in which students come into the college and at the point of entry become either certificate or degree students. There can be an element of parallelism between the two courses in the first year; indeed there can be an element of common teaching, but we think if these are going to be distinctive awards, it shouldn't be complete identity. If at the end of the first year, the students on the certificate have performed at a high level, a level which is judged to be broadly equivalent to that of the students following the degree route, then the Council is quite prepared to see methods for transferring students over at the end of the first year from the certificate on to the degree. Another method which seems to be finding some favour is that in which year one of the certificate might be described as year nought of the degree, in which the students come in and take year one of the certificate and if they achieve a high enough standard they then transfer over to year one of the degree. In this way they take four years to a degree, and if they are good enough, five years to an honours degree. Strangely enough the DES seems to feel that the grant regulations don't need to present insuperable difficulties to that particular solution and we are looking at it in one or two colleges. So, our objective is again to maintain standards and those examples are two of the patterns which are being used to do that in a number of institutions.

If I may turn now to in-service education, there certainly have been a number of very interesting courses proposed to us, in which the in-service B. Ed is seen as radically different from the B. Ed taken by the eighteen plus student, in which there is a real partnership developed between the school, the authority and the college. Indeed, it can be said that the school is almost seen as a laboratory associated with the course. We have got some very valuable experiments there and one only hopes that the current economic difficulties will not prevent these courses from running and from proving their great value over a number of years. I don't want to say much about these and other in-service courses; indeed, one can't say much about them because I think this is one of the development areas that we still have to do a lot of work on in association with the colleges. We certainly wish to assist colleges by validating diplomas and masters degrees and providing a range of awards for in-service work, but we don't see a clear picture yet and I think this is one thing that we will want to discuss thoroughly with the colleges and the universities, so that we can see how this will develop and clarify.

My final point is a few words on diversification. One of the major problems as we see it is the assumption that has been made by the DES, and which is made explicit in Circular 6/74, that course units should be devised in common for both a BA and a B. Ed. That colleges who want to propose courses under Circular 6/74 are required to demonstrate that they have used these common units, especially tailored for a B. Ed building in a planned relationship between professional and academic studies, that you can then just take a group of these modules, re-jig them and say that that is a BA. It does not appear to be self-evident to us that staff who are excellent at their job of teaching B. Eds and who have got their experience through years of teaching in schools are automatically going to be able to teach honours BA degrees in French or English or mathematics. Although we have tremendous sympathy for the problems in the colleges, to believe that this concept that units can be re-ordered in this way just doesn't work like that. Of course there can be common units, but to think that you can assemble courses from nothing other than those common units is a different thing and we haven't seen many examples where this is successful yet. Another aspect of this problem is that many of the B. Eds are big courses with large intakes, with many options within them. Colleges, understandably, almost encouraged by the DES in Circular 6/74, try to put exactly the same variety of options in a BA course, and then get alarmed when the Council points out that they shouldn't do it that way, that they should concentrate on their real strengths, and then they will get more experience and can broaden out from there.

Finally, I would say that diversification really should be working out new opportunities in the colleges, not just duplicating courses which already exist rather than something which is entirely new. But none-the-less, if we are trying to offer a range of opportunities for students, then we should try to plan some of the new things.

# Curriculum development in higher education

Anthony Becher

Teacher educators have more to gain by hanging together than by hanging separately; but I much doubt whether overall policy committees (of the type exemplified by UCET) represent the best form of togetherness. I would argue in favour of functional collaboration in curriculum development, rather than for structural collaboration (of the kind typified by discussions about how many contact hours should define a Dip. H. E. or how many years it would properly take to earn an Honours B. Ed starting from one B and one E at A level and Cs in both mathematics and English at O level). In reviewing some possibilities for collective action among teacher educators, I would like first to focus attention on projects which involve groups of teachers in different institutions. It may be noted that, despite their common starting points, many of these schemes end with individual curricula in each participating institution. Then I want to take a contrasting view, and look at attempts to develop the curriculum within an individual college, university or polytechnic. It should not go unremarked that despite their diverse starting points, some of these initiatives result in common curriculum elements in a number of different contexts. I shall draw my examples mainly from curriculum developments in universities, because that is the field with which I happen to be most familiar. Of course, it could be objected that colleges have plenty of other things to occupy them without concerning themselves with the curriculum problems of others. It might indeed be questioned whether the curriculum is of much importance anyway, when so many colleges have more far-reaching institutional issues to worry about. As against this, my own view (which reflects those put forward by William Percival and Norman Evans) is that changes in institutional structure are in one sense educationally irrelevant. They are obviously important in political terms to ministers, civil servants and local authorities, and they are obviously important in human terms to those who work in the institutions concerned. But they do not necessarily affect the nature and the quality of the education that goes on within those institutions. In terms of the learner's needs, the curriculum process matters a good deal more than the management pattern. So I would like to open up a debate on new curricular patterns, rather than add yet another comment to the seemingly endless discussion of new organisational problems. Although I must do so in large measure obliquely, through examples of recent developments in other academic fields, I hope some of my examples may be recognisably relevant to the interests of teacher educators.

In my background notes (see Appendix) I argue that there are certain inherent distinctions between curriculum development in higher education and curriculum development in schools. The difference which is most significant for the colleges is not so much in the characteristics of the teachers as in the absence of common external examination constraints. As a result, colleges are freer in many ways than schools to identify their own curriculum aims. Although this is an obvious advantage, it inevitably makes it more difficult to engage in large-scale common curriculum development. It also suggests that the model of the Schools Council as a mechanism for curriculum collaboration may not be a very appropriate one for higher education in general or teacher education in particular. What would offer the right kind of co-ordinating structure is a question that may well deserve some of the sustained thought and imaginative energy which the higher education system has so far chosen to deflect in other directions.

Despite the obvious difficulties, there are nevertheless some things to be said about inter-institutional collaboration in curriculum design.

As I have suggested, one has to start with the acceptance that, as far as higher education is concerned, individual departments in a given subject area are very much more idiosyncratic than they are at the school level. Because of this variation in the nature and aims of the curricula in different institutions, anyone who sets out to stimulate co-operative development has first and foremost to recognise the need for adaptability to the individual circumstances of any participating departments. There have been about a dozen fairly sizeable inter-institutional projects of one kind or another set up with external funding in the past five or six years in higher education. Looking at them collectively, it is possible to distinguish three main styles of approach. Of course, many schemes are an amalgam of those styles; but it may be useful to regard the styles themselves as three dimensions against which the position of any particular project could be plotted. In what follows, I will give brief examples which represent points on each dimension in turn. Incidentally, the sets of characteristics which I shall attempt to identify at the higher education level are also reflected in similar contrasts at the school level. One handy way of labelling them is by adapting the terminology which Donald Schon put forward in his 1970 Reith lectures; so I shall call the styles in question the centre-periphery, the periphery-centre and the periphery-periphery. In this context, the centre symbolises the development team and the periphery symbolises their clients; the contrasts lie in the differing relationships between the one and the other.

Let us look first at the approach which is closest in its character to the original curriculum development model adopted by Nuffield Science and by the early Schools Council projects, such as the Modern Languages Project. Here the flow of development runs from the centre to the periphery. The emphasis is on producing carefully-structured, high quality teaching and learning materials, on testing them out in a number of different institutions, and then on revising them in the light of these trials before making them generally available. The development work is usually done by a fairly close-knit central team, somewhat on Open University pattern. The demands of adaptability impose two main constraints on the types of materials which can be produced in higher education on the basis of this model. The first is that they are usually limited to marginal areas of the curriculum where no strong departmental claims have been staked out: for example, remedial programmes, service courses, courses on laboratory techniques - the kind of things that nobody particularly wants to teach - or courses in newly-established subject areas. The second constraint is related to this: the resulting products tend to be, if not 'teacher-proof', at any rate designed not to involve the teacher very closely. They often take the form of independent learning materials designed for students to work at on their own.

One of the main archetypes of this particular pattern of development is the Joint University Genetics Project, in which - significantly - the Open University Science faculty is the major participant The aim is to produce an introductory genetics course which will be adaptable for use in a variety of different institutions, based on a set of packages of the general type which the Open University has now made familiar. There are also a number of more localised and smaller-scale variants of this centre-periphery approach, where two or more departments from different institutions get together to design common curricula elements. One interesting example is provided by the chemistry departments of Chelsea College and Cardiff University, where the staff have collectively designed a scheme for teaching chemical thermodynamics which they both use in a virtually identical way.

The main feature, then, of the centre-periphery approach is the central creation of fairly substantial modules of tightly-organised course materials. But the demands of adaptability have also given rise to alternative approaches - for example, by loosening the structure both of the curriculum materials and of the development team itself. At the school level, the Sixth Form General Studies Project was one of the schemes which adopted this more open pattern of operation, reversing the flow of development so that it ran from the periphery to the centre. In the periphery-centre approach the emphasis is on involving large numbers of contributing practitioners: there is usually a small central team, whose function is largely organisational and editorial. The materials are usually collected thematically, rather than offered as a series of pre-planned curricula sequences. That is, they are not designed to give a comprehensive coverage of any topic, but to serve as a resource bank on which teachers and students can draw. In keeping with the openness of structure, the emphasis is generally on materials for group discussion rather than on materials for independent study. The prototype of this approach at the higher education level, the Science Teacher Education Project, was pioneered by the science tutors in colleges and departments of education. It involved the collaboration of some hundred science tutors in various parts of the country, who formed themselves into nine or ten topic groups. Each group contributed and commissioned items of material relevant to its own topic, which the central team edited. The resulting resource collections were then tried out and re-edited in the light of users' comments. The resulting materials were published in the autumn of 1974, and have attracted considerable interest both at home and overseas. There are now quite a few other somewhat less ambitious schemes to exchange individual items of curriculum material between different institutions of higher education: one example is provided by the Centre for Learning Materials in Medical Education, run under the auspices of the British Medical Association. The style of curriculum development exemplified by such schemes is of course in marked contrast with that of the centre-periphery approach described earlier. Its products are teacher-dependent rather than directly aimed at the learner. The emphasis is on assembling several relatively small modules rather than on designing a few large and fairly elaborate ones. In effect, it offers its clients a do-it-yourself kit for curriculum design rather than a ready-made finished product.

Both these approaches, in their different ways, put the main emphasis on the preparation of written or audio-visual materials, or both. But the third style which I want to discuss differs from each of them in its concern with the process of teaching and learning, and its relegation of the developmental products - the curriculum materials themselves - to an incidental and subsidiary role. At the school level, the pattern for this approach was set by the Humanities Curriculum Project which concentrated on promoting the flow of development from one point on the periphery to another. A central team which adopts the periphery-periphery model acts less as a production or editorial unit than as a stimulator of new educational practices, a monitor of their effects, and a communicator of the resulting ideas and experience. There is a strong emphasis on in-service teacher education and on the establishment of a new teaching tradition, and relatively little emphasis on specific items of curricular content. Such an approach may lend itself particularly well to higher education. In the first place, it does not pose any obvious threat to the teacher's command over his subject-matter; and that is something I would argue (see Appendix) to be an important part of his professional identity, which is challenged explicitly by centre-periphery, and implicitly by periphery-centre, schemes. In the second place, it offers the kind of help in developing teaching techniques which many academic staff now recognise that they need.

Perhaps the project which most clearly exemplifies this periphery-periphery style is the Higher Education Learning Project (Physics). Even before its work had reached an advanced stage, it was clear that it had succeeded in attracting considerable interest from physics departments in universities and polytechnics. The project team's activities include, for example, disseminating ideas for 'skills training sessions' in science tutorials, developing methods of running seminar groups in physics, and promulgating experience with various forms of independent study. More localised counterparts of this type of approach can be found in some of the recently-established staff development programmes which involve groups of specialist teachers from various institutions, and in the work of the relatively few existing teachers' centres in the higher education sector.

All three of the approaches I have briefly characterised - centre-periphery, periphery-centre and periphery-periphery - have, of course, their inherent advantages and disadvantages. If groups of teacher educators (or, for that matter, groups of engineers, groups of biologists, or groups of teachers of Italian) come to a view that it would be useful for them to collaborate in curriculum design, all three styles could provide them with viable possibilities on which to base their work. It is certainly pointless to prescribe any one formula, or even to suggest some ideal amalgam of all three. What is likely to serve as the best model for a particular programme must depend on the context in which it is to be developed - on the institutions concerned, on the subject-matter, on the objects of the exercise, and on the resources likely to be available. But at least no collaborative scheme now has to start altogether from first principles: there is a considerable fund of experience and know-how within the educational system on which those embarking on a new venture can draw. If they are too vain, or idle, or foolhardy to do so, they will surely deserve the consequent penalty of having to learn from their own mistakes rather than from the hard-won successes of their predecessors.

Having so far concentrated on forms of inter-institutional development, I would like now to turn attention to some of the main patterns of curricular change in individual departments. Again, although my examples are drawn largely from universities, I hope they may suggest possibilities for future curriculum innovations in teacher education. It is perhaps worth emphasising at the outset that, despite the almost perverse isolationism of many higher education institutions, a remarkable amount of change in the nature and content of undergraduate teaching has taken place over the last few years. It is, as one might expect, evolutionary and incremental rather than revolutionary; ad hoc and patchy rather than systematic. There are nevertheless several common strands which run through the fabric; it may help, in picking them out, to divide them into three main categories. The first is concerned with the overall organisation of the system; the second relates to curriculum structures; and third centres on new approaches to teaching, learning and assessment. Before considering each of these in turn, there are two general points to be made. Firstly, change is by no means confined to, nor is it noticeably more pervasive in, new institutions - indeed, some of the older-established universities have shown themselves to be surprisingly innovative in terms of the undergraduate curriculum. The second noticeable feature - which is in marked contrast with changes at the school level - is that curriculum structures and teaching/learning approaches tend to be totally divorced from one another (in other words, new curricular patterns very often co-exist with traditional teaching methods, and new teaching methods are usually developed within traditional curriculum patterns).

I shall deal only briefly with organisational changes because, as I have argued earlier, they are not themselves a genuine form of development - even though they may sometimes create the pre-conditions for curricular innovation. Most of the major reforms in organisational structure over the past decade have of course taken place in the public sector, and have thus affected the polytechnics and the colleges rather than the universities. Their main impact on the curriculum has been made through new systems of assessment and validation. The results are widely known and reasonably well documented, in the form of accounts of new CNAA degrees in the polytechnics, the development of B. Ed curricula in the colleges, and programmes for the Dip. H. E. in both. Such structural changes as there have been in the university system have stemmed from the creation of new institutions: the post-Robbins universities, the ex-CATs and, more recently, the Open University. Among the new universities, Sussex, East Anglia and the New University of Ulster opted for a pattern of academic management grounded on broadly-based schools of studies rather than on the traditional discipline-centred departments. The resulting reduction in the power of specialist interest groups has (as originally intended) encouraged the development of a substantial range of interdisciplinary degree courses. In many of the ex-CATs, the tradition of sandwich courses which they imported into the university sector has encouraged a more vocational and practical emphasis in the undergraduate curriculum; and the fact that the science students on which they largely depend have proved so hard to attract has stimulated considerable rethinking of conventional teaching approaches. The Open University has in a remarkably short time established itself as an institution with much to offer to those concerned with curriculum development in higher education. The special problems which it had to tackle, of teaching-at-a-distance, gave rise to a series of innovative techniques. Some of them - such as the establishment of course teams, the development of highly sophisticated independent learning materials, and the systematic application of ideas drawn from educational technology - have had a far-reaching influence on other universities, and on many polytechnics and colleges.

Turning now to my second category, of changes in curriculum structures, the developments which I want briefly to characterise need to be seen against the background of the traditional single-subject three-year honours course. There are three noticeable groups of changes (it is surprising how often innovative categories seem to come in triplets). The first represents a move towards less specialised education: the Keele Foundation Year offers one familiar example, and another is provided by the older-established Scottish universities in their multi-disciplinary first year courses But the shift from a narrow to a wide range of curricular content has become more noticeable in recent years as a result of the steady growth of combined and joint honours degrees in many universities Another form of broadening has also begun to manifest itself in the context of professional qualifications: for example, a number of medical schools have introduced community medicine, medical sociology or the study of behavioural science as a broader educational element in the curriculum; some law schools have similarly introduced a component designed to set the law in its social context; and there are now several courses on the theme of the engineer and society (many of them actively stimulated by the professional engineering institutions).

There is also a distinct - though loosely-related - tendency towards interdisciplinary studies The emphasis, in this group of innovative curricula, is on integration between two or more disciplines rather than (as in the cases of broader academic or professional courses) merely on the juxtaposition of different subjects. The notion of interdisciplinarity is often linked with the demand for 'relevance'. It has given rise to a number of courses based on themes or problems which are seen as socially relevant or as reflecting the pressing personal concerns of students. The recent development of interdisciplinary curricula has been remarkable both for its rapidity and for its pervasiveness. It is not confined to one group of disciplines, but spans the whole range. One can find examples in the humanities, not only in courses such as European Studies, which a number of universities (including Loughborough, Sussex and UMIST) have recently introduced, but also in combinations of, or attempted integrations between, literature and philosophy, or history and literature. There are instances in the social sciences, in courses on Development Studies (at East Anglia and Sussex), or in integrated courses (as at Birmingham and York) on the methodology of the social sciences as a whole rather than on the curricular content of any one branch. A number of science faculties (Ulster, East Anglia and Sheffield) now offer courses on the environmental sciences, and one or two provide degree programmes on energy studies, or on human sciences; while some of the recent developments in technology are designed to integrate the concepts of engineering and management (examples include courses at City University and Strathclyde), or to bring different disciplines to bear on the problems of urban planning.

A third trend contrasts, in its underlying philosophy, with the rationale behind the development of interdisciplinary programmes. It is characterised by a move towards unit course structures, either within a single disciplinary area (as in the University of London, where the science faculties were the first to adopt a unit scheme in the late 1960's, although only one or two non-science departments in its individual colleges have done so since); or else across the science/arts boundary (as in the Polytechnic of Central London); or across the whole range of academic subjects (as in the case of City Polytechnic)  The main aim, in these unit or modular degree programmes, is to allow students greater freedom of choice: to present them with an a la carte menu rather than a traditional table d'hote menu. Schemes of this kind have some similarity to the course credit system which is a familiar feature of American higher education, though in practice academics in this country have shied away from a totally laissez-faire system. One usually finds that there are a number of carefully-planned constraints on choice, and that a sizeable proportion of advanced courses have their own prerequisites at a more elementary level. Most schemes have also developed fairly elaborate counselling arrangements to help students choose combinations of units which together make up some sort of coherent entity. Even so, the integration of the different components of study is not - and (given the variety of possible routes through the system) could not be - the overriding concern of curricula based on this pattern. They are atomistic and rationalist in their view of knowledge, where interdisciplinary courses are organic and romantic.

Each of these alternative curricular patterns - broader courses, interdisciplinary programmes and unit schemes - has some potential relevance to teacher education. For example, the difficulties of working out an interdisciplinary curriculum are not so very different from the problems posed by designing an integrated concurrent course. Experience in developing unit structures is relevant to those colleges who have adopted a consecutive pattern, and particularly those who are amalgamating with a polytechnic which already has a modular system. And the techniques of planning broader courses may well be applicable to situations in which the teacher educator is concerned to keep the student's options open, as well as the situations in which a need is seen to set professional skills in their wider social context.

My third main category of curricular changes in higher education relates to the day-to-day business of teaching, learning and assessment. Here, the most noticeable characteristic seems to be a concern to help students develop a greater autonomy in their learning. One might almost say that the old colonialism of the intellect, under which a young man would come and sit as an apprentice beside the established scholar, pick up what he could and go away again, is now giving way to the less paternalistic notion of a commonwealth of knowledge in which students are deliberately encouraged to become self-determining individuals, capable of continuing to learn throughout the rest of their lives. This analogy seems, at least, to be the most straightforward way of accounting for the marked emphasis in recent years on independent learning programmes, such as those in the biochemistry department at Dundee or the engineering department at Exeter, where self-study materials have largely replaced the traditional didactic lecture, and where the main staff-student contact takes the form of tutorials in which known factual material can be critically discussed and put in a wider context. It may also help to explain the considerable growth of co-operative learning through small group work which has become a noticeable feature of both arts and science courses. (East Anglia, as one of the pioneers of this development, has acquired a sophistication in running seminar courses which puts it ahead of most other institutions, but many of them are rapidly gaining ground). The notion of a new commonwealth of knowledge may also help to put in perspective the otherwise extraordinary increase in the number of science courses which now make a feature of individual and group project work, and the increasing proportion of arts courses which give prominence to student dissertations.

Alongside the many changes in the nature of the learning activity in which students are now expected to engage, there are accompanying innovations in assessment procedure. Many of them appear - whether consciously or unconsciously - to have been introduced to allow for the different learning styles of individual students. The vogue some four or five years ago for continuous assessment now seems to have given way to a greater variety of choice. Where a degree course includes project work or dissertations, these are rightly taken into account, since they invariably involve a great deal of effort on the part of the student. There have been a number of experiments with open book examinations (in which students are allowed to consult references), and with seen examinations (in which students are given the questions some days beforehand). A number of departments (and perhaps notably in chemistry and medicine) have experimented with multiple choice and short answer questions; and viva voce examinations (which represent an old tradition in continental universities) have been introduced as further variants on the conventional pattern of three-hour unseen essay papers. Some departments explicitly provide their students with a choice of the forms of assessment to which they wish to submit themselves; one or two allow students to negotiate with their examiners about their grades; and one department - the School of Architecture at Birmingham Polytechnic - issues a profile in the place of a classified degree. But even leaving aside the more far-reaching changes in the way the students' capabilities are ascertained, there are a substantial number of departments in which non-traditional assessment now counts for about fifty per cent of the total degree mark.

Although it may well be the case that many colleges are further ahead than the universities and polytechnics in the development of new curricular structures or new modes of teaching, learning and assessment, they surely must have much to gain, and little to lose, by sharing their experience of common approaches At the moment, one of the most absurd and wasteful, features of the higher education system is that so many people seem prepared to busy themselves re-inventing the wheel. It is extraordinary how many curricular concerns are common to different institutions; in one place after another one can find, for example, interdisciplinary courses, or project work, or new approaches to small group teaching. It is all the more remarkable that such developments are so pervasive, in that the teachers concerned in bringing them about very seldom know of each other's existence. It has been one of the concerns of the Nuffield Higher Education Group to put like-minded innovators in touch with one another. To this end, the Group has organised a series of working conferences on such themes as independence in learning, small group teaching, and new assessment techniques. Those who attended, though they were from a wide diversity of subject backgrounds, found a great deal in common. They were able to learn from each others' successes and failures and, perhaps even more important, showed a readiness to support each others' endeavours in what was often a fairly hostile environment.

I have probably said more than enough already to make my prejudices plain. Perhaps I should end by asserting my conviction that it is only by sharing curriculum concerns, and building collaborative activities on them, that teachers in higher education (and teacher educators among the rest)

will manage to break down the educationally indefensible barriers which
have been erected between institutions by those who see themselves as
our political overlords and administrative masters. If the binary boundary
is one day shown up as the meaningless farce I believe it to be, it will be
done by the collective action of teachers in redesigning the basic fabric
of the educational process - that is, the curriculum itself.

# Appendix

SOME CONTRASTS BETWEEN SCHOOLS AND HIGHER EDUCATION

Systematic curriculum development at the school level has been taking
place for more than a decade. It began early in 1962 with the initiation
of the various Nuffield Science projects, and has steadily gathered
momentum (first under the auspices of the Nuffield Foundation and later
under the aegis of the Schools Council) ever since. The problems and
possibilities of work in this genre are by now well known and widely
documented.

In contrast the notion of designing a new curriculum in the higher
education sector is a relatively unfamiliar one. This is not of course
to say that curricular change never occurs. In fact, the Nuffield Higher
Education Group's current study (1975) suggests that it is a good deal
more widespread than one might expect from the general image of a highly
conservative academic profession. But the revision of existing courses,
and the generation of new ones, do tend to take place in a fairly haphazard
and ad hoc way; so much so that one is in general inclined to speak of
them as examples of curriculum evolution rather than of development or
design.

Why is this so? What is there to explain the apparently marked
contrast between the nature of curricular change in the primary and
secondary schools and that in the universities, polytechnics and colleges

of education?   Two points of difference are fairly obvious; both may help towards solving the enigma.

One lies in a marked distinction in the mechanisms for curricular control.  By tradition, each school is free to determine its own curriculum, and the myth of 'the freedeom of the teacher' is as jealously guarded as is the corresponding myth in higher education of 'academic autonomy'. But in practice, public examinations exercise powerful constraints on what the secondary schools can undertake in the way of curricular experiment.   The effect of GCE and CSE syllabuses is to impose a remarkable degree of uniformity on courses at the secondary level;  and - despite the theoretical options of Mode 3 examinations - most teachers seem to prefer the confining security of a defined curricular pattern to the uncertain liberty of a do-it-yourself educational programme.  Such limitations on freedom are reinforced by the nature of the available textbooks: quite justifiably educational publishers give preference to those works which fit in with existing examination requirements, rather than to those which radically challenge them.   Even at the primary level, the same constraints operate in an attenuated form.  The demands of secondary schools exercise a 'backwash effect';  they are given substance by an understandable concern on the part of parents and of the community at large that pupils should emerge from primary education at least reasonably literate and moderately numerate.   Best-selling authors, particularly of books on elementary English and elementary mathematics, help to strengthen the sense of uniformity created by well-advertised trends in pedagogic fashion.

Given this relative degree of homogeneity in school curricula, the systematic development of innovative programmes is a relatively straightforward business.   Projects in any subject area have necessarily to begin by creating new standard texts.   The next step is to persuade the appropriate examining agencies to set alternative examinations embodying the new curricular aims.   Once these tasks are successfully completed, there remains the much more difficult business of creating a teaching tradition to match  . . .  but at least the reformed curriculum has now its place on the map.

In contrast, there are no common curricular goals for the higher education sector. Degrees of academic independence do of course vary. A university department determines its own curriculum in very large measure, and (except in law, medicine or engineering, where professional bodies exercise a modest watchdog function) is able to set its own examinations, subject to the scrutiny of an external examiner of its own choice. The polytechnics, and some colleges, are dependent on the external validation of the CNAA; other colleges are beholden to a neighbouring university for the approval of their courses and the acceptance of their qualifications. But in no case does such validation require the same degree of curricular uniformity as is imposed on the schools. The result is that curricular patterns are far more diverse in tertiary than in primary or secondary institutions; and hence any attempt to generate new possibilities at a national level is bound to run into difficulties even more intractable than those encountered by school development programmes.

The second significant difference between the schools and higher education lies in the characteristic distinctions between their teachers. At the school level, staff tend to identify themselves more strongly with the process of education than with the content of their specialist fields. They are open to arguments based on pedagogical premises, and do not consider themselves first and foremost as guardians (or even rulers) of territories of knowledge. They are prepared, by their professional training, to entertain new ideas about how young people learn; and they are also ready to take guidance, from those more closely in touch with current research in their own parent disciplines, about the changes in subject matter and the developments in conceptual framework which should be properly embodied in an up-to-date treatment of a given theme. So if a new curriculum programme offers a persuasive rationale in terms of teaching approach, and an authoritative statement about the current methodology of the subject, the schools are willing in principle to take it seriously.

The large mass of teachers in higher education have exactly the opposite priorities. Few of them (the staff of colleges of education are exceptional in this) have undergone any formal pedagogic training. Most of them have, however, undertaken a rigorous and highly specialised training in research. They thus regard themselves first and foremost as experts in subject-matter, but only secondarily - and often in a rather minor and amateur way - as people concerned with the facilitation of learning. So they tend to be deaf to arguments both about improvements in teaching approach (which they regard as largely irrelevant) and about modifications in the content and structuring of knowledge (in which their own expertise is by definition paramount). It is scarcely surprising that curriculum development, in the form which has now become a familiar feature of the school scene, has gained few footholds on the unyielding surfaces which lie beyond the barrier of the A level examination.

**REFERENCES**

Nuffield Foundation, The (1975) The Drift of Change, an Interim Report of the Group for Research and Innovation in Higher Education, London, The Nuffield Foundation

# Modular course structures in higher education

**Kenneth Gardner**

A module is an amount of student work. In the absence of a more appropriate unit, it is measured in terms of time, say sixty hours or six hours per week per ten week term. The sixty hours may be divided into contact time and students' own work. The extreme form of a modular system is based on a variety of self-contained modules from which a student may select his programme in any mix or order which seems to him appropriate. Each module is assessed separately and the final grade is the average of the grades accumulated for each module. At the other end of the scale, a linear structure would submit a given group of students to a single course without options with assessment largely at the end. In practice neither of these extremes would be entirely acceptable in our higher education system today. The extreme modular course is modified by the constraints of the timetable and the need for educational and professional coherence. The pure linear course is softened by a choice of options and various manifestations of continuous assessment. Also, for the sake of convenience, most linear courses are divided into term-sized units which have a distinctly modular flavour. It is therefore the intention of this paper to postulate a continuum of course patterns varying from extreme modular to extreme linear and to test the hypothesis by examining the central area where the split between the two may be found if it exists. Examples will be chosen from a point of view of a teacher education institution with a brief to diversify.

Good modular systems, whilst emphasising a student's freedom of choice, make considerable provision for academic guidance both at the start of a course, when a student makes his initial selection of modules, and later when there is need for further choice or a change of direction. The weight of such guidance will vary from scheme to scheme and indeed from student to student, but students will, on the whole, tend to accept guidance at least at the beginning of their course. Such guidance will on the whole tend to direct students along relatively familiar paths which have proved to be satisfactory over a period of years. This is inevitable, and probably desirable, but in practice consioerably limits the flexibility of the system. A student intending to teach in, say, a first school must of necessity take modules in such topics as child development, teaching of reading and teaching of number. There can be some choice within these professional modules but there is an essential bare minimum usually called the 'core'. Such a core presumably exists in engineering, business studies, accountancy, librarianship and other professionally oriented courses. The existence of a core provides another constraint on a modular system.

Educational coherence is a difficult topic for discussion because it has intuitive meaning and is not easy to define. It is however central to our debate. A well-designed linear course has coherence. A student taking the earlier part can be referred with confidence to what is coming later. Later work can build on concepts and skills developed earlier and hopefully retained. Whilst in some cases this is merely desirable, in others it is absolutely necessary. It is not usually feasible, for example, to take a course on differential equations until the techniques of basic integration have been mastered. The concept of coherence may however be treated more subtly. For example, a course on history may be designed to emphasise the effects of the characters of prominent politicians upon the decision of their day. Such a course may last through several modules but the content would be designed to interrelate, and the emphases would be the same throughout. Thus the whole set of modules would need to be designed as an entity and studied as an entity for the best educational benefit. The modular solution to these problems is to specify pre-requisites for each module. For example, module seven could not be taken until modules one and three had been completed. There are, however, problems. If it is necessary to stipulate that module seven could not be taken until modules one to six inclusive had been completed in that order to preserve educational coherence, then we have merely reached a linear pattern by a more tortuous route. If, on the other hand, module seven may be taken once either modules one, three or five have been completed, then there is the risk that, in trying to allow for a variety of student programmes, much may be lost in educational coherence. The latter situation obtains at the moment with students entering a higher education course in, say, mathematics with a variety of different A level backgrounds. The outcome is something less than satisfactory.

The question of coherence may however be tackled from a different point of view. Granted that a modular structure has a lack of coherence as a potential weakness, it is possible to remedy this by building in such activities as projects, special studies, case studies and professional experience. It is probable that the coherence difficulty may be overcome by these methods, but the methods themselves provide further restrictions on the flexibility of the system.

In a well-designed linear course, the work reaches a consistently higher standard as the course progresses. This must also be the case within a modular framework. A system of pre-requisites is some help here, but in practice it is necessary to provide some restrictions as to the range of introductory or foundation modules which may be taken so that on the one hand students get an adequate background for later, more specialised work, whilst on the other, students do not sacrifice depth to excessive breadth. At the other end of the scale, students usually need to take a sufficient number of modules at honours degree level to merit that award.

The restrictions so far has been on academic or professional grounds. A major factor however is that there can never be complete freedom of choice in selecting modules unless student numbers are so large that most modules are repeated possibly several times each. In practice this tends to reinforce more orthodox and acceptable course patterns. Of course, the smaller the institution, the less possibility there is of repeating modules and the greater the restrictions of timetable limitations.

The previous section demonstrates that the flexibility of a modular structure is badly restricted by the various educational and administrative pressures upon it. Here I would like to investigate what, if anything, is left once these pressures have been assimilated or accommodated.

If one considers course patterns one can see that the traditional pattern in teacher education has been that a student takes a main subject, educational theory and professional studies. In general the amount of time devoted to the main subject and theory of education has been fixed with some modest flexibility across the age ranges with regard to professional work. The pattern has however presented difficulties. For example, in view of the shortage of mathematics and science teachers, a student who aims to teach these subjects in a secondary school needs all the mathematics and science he can get. He is unlikely to teach anything else and will be of most value to his intended profession if he concentrates on his specialisms with a relative lack of emphasis elsewhere. On the other hand, a student intending to teach infants may prefer to reduce her main course commitment to a minimum, or choose several 'main courses' aiming for breadth rather than depth, or devote 'main course' time to a study of child development in depth. In a modular system, even bearing in mind the problems of 'core' studies and levels of work, it should be possible to go some way towards accommodating the various types of student preference. Such flexibility will be even more desirable in diversified areas where the restrictions of professional needs may not be involved although care needs to be taken to avoid fragmentation.

If one considers student intake within a modular framework it is possible for, say, geographers, biologists, business study students and mathemeticians to take the same introductory course in statistics. It can be argued that this is a good thing, since it allows for a cross-fertilisation of ideas, insights and experience. On the other hand, the students will form a heterogeneous group with a variety of mathematical

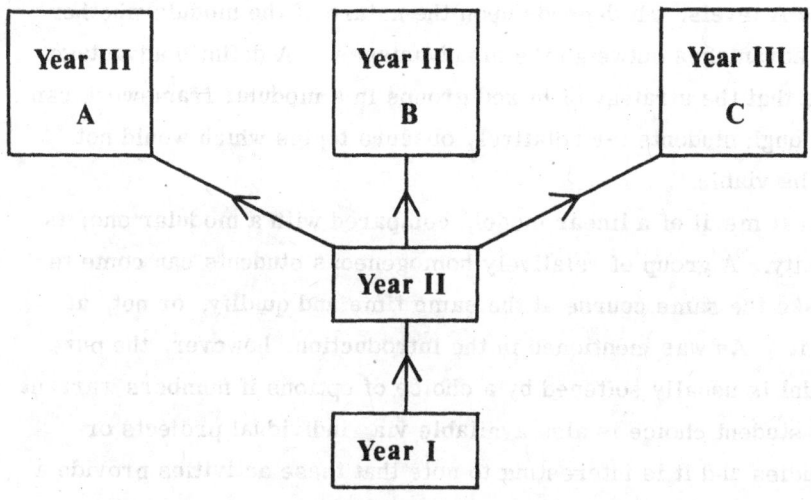

**Figure 1  A Linear System**

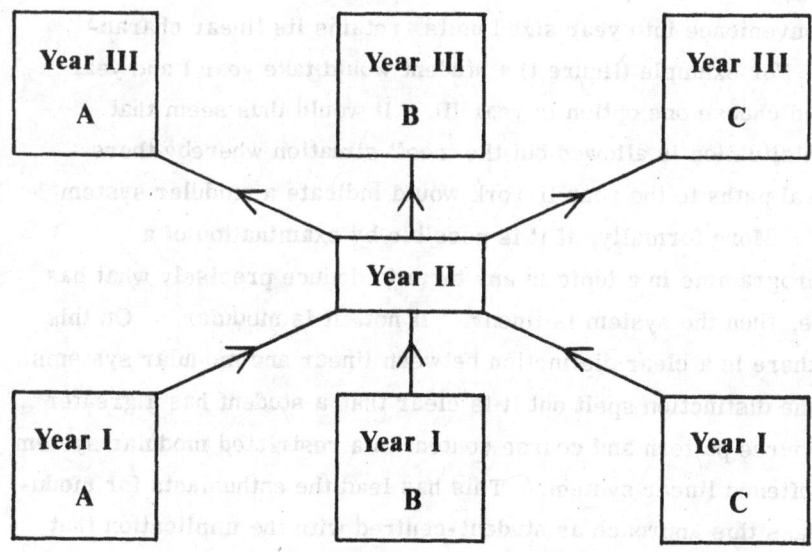

**Figure 2  A Modular System**

backgrounds, varying from O level (which could be made a pre-requisite) to two good A levels. It depends upon the nature of the module whether or not the advantages outweigh the disadvantages. A definite advantage however is that the strategy of mixed groups in a modular framework can produce enough students for relatively obscure topics which would not otherwise be viable.

The great merit of a linear model, compared with a modular one, is its simplicity. A group of relatively homogeneous students can come to college, take the same course at the same time and qualify, or not, at the end of it. As was mentioned in the introduction, however, the pure linear model is usually softened by a choice of options if numbers warrant it. Some student choice is also available via individual projects or special studies and it is interesting to note that these activities provide a softening influence in the linear model whereas they are linked with educational or vocational coherence in the modular system and are a restricting force.

It is suggested that even the most softened form of a linear model, split for convenience into year sized units, retains its linear characteristics. For example (figure 1) a student would take year I and year II 'core' and choose one option in year III. It would thus seem that the 'branch' situation is allowed but the 'root' situation whereby there were several paths to the year II work would indicate a modular system (figure 2). More formally, if it is possible by examination of a student's programme in a topic in any term to deduce precisely what has gone before, then the system is linear. If not, it is modular. On this definition there is a clear distinction between linear and modular systems.

From the distinction spelt out it is clear that a student has a greater choice of course pattern and course content in a restricted modular system than in a softened linear system. This has lead the enthusiasts for modularity to class this approach as student-centred with the implication that the traditional linear courses are not. Modular courses are certainly student-centred in the sense that, with greater flexibility, the student has more responsibility for planning his own course, under guidance, than in a linear system. The price is paid, however, in that individual modules are less likely to fit a particular student's needs and a student's programme of modules is less likely to hang together as a coherent whole. Indeed, it becomes clear that as the modules are made more flexible in the varieties of students that can use them the less specifically can they be tailored to particular purposes. For example, a course cannot be aimed specifically at third year students when it is not likely that all students will come from the third year. Indeed, it can be seen that as the ability to use a module flexibly increases, then the degree of specificity in the 'aiming' of the module at a particular student audience diminishes - there is a direct relationship (ie, for mathemeticians $f \times s = K$). Similarly as flexibility in the modular course increases so the less it is likely that the student's route will form a coherent whole (ie, $f \times c = K$). Since flexibility, specificity and coherence are all valid educational aims in the construction of an academic pattern, however, the solution must be some form of compromise between the three. In the present teacher education situation the scales would seem to be tipped in favour of the restricted modular approach. The cutback in student numbers means that institutions can only sustain their present variety of main courses and continue to offer varied programmes by educating prospective teachers and other students within the same framework. This is only possible using a modular system if viable groups are to be maintained.

The aims of a modular pattern of courses can only be expressed in very general terms. The aims for a specific linear course may be more precise but are still at a high level of generality. In the modular situation, however, it is possible to produce specific objectives for each module which may be tested with a much higher degree of accuracy. As mentioned earlier, therefore, the standard pattern of assessment for a modular programme is to test each module separately and to average out the grades to produce a final mark. This contrasts remarkably with the traditional means of assessment of linear courses which is by final examination. Even where the linear model is softened by projects or special studies, they tend to be started late in the course so that the weight of assessment is towards the end rather than spread evenly throughout.

The nature of the assessment procedure, however, should be decided on educational rather than structural grounds. There are good reasons for having assessment procedures where the emphasis is towards the end of the course. It is a student's standard at the end which is important, not that at the beginning. The late developer should not be penalised unduly because of early inadequacies since, apart from other considerations, this can only dampen his will to succeed. On the other hand, the disadvantages of a final examination system are well known. A few final examination papers cannot assess the whole of three years work and inevitably an element of luck is involved. Many students react badly to the pressures of examination conditions. Also the examination system is not the most appropriate means of assessing many aspects of students' work. Assessment of individual modules, however, also presents its difficulties. The acute pressures of the final examination become the chronic pressures of continuous assessment and the focus for each module becomes the grade to be awarded rather than the educational content. Fundamentally assessment procedures are inconvenient but necessary and even provide their own motivating force when all else fails. There is no final solution to the assessment problem and it is necessary to adopt the best compromise available.

It is reasonable to suggest that mastery of content is best assessed module by module since the content is clearly specified and the element of luck inherent in final examination and the need for excessive last minute revision are both avoided. The content tends to be more complex towards the end of a course, however, so that it is reasonable to use some form of weighted average when combining grades so as to emphasise the later modules. Higher level skills are however best tested towards the end of a course so that they will have had time to develop using individual studies and final examinations so as to satisfy all varieties of temperament. If these arguments are accepted, the modular system has the edge since it is possible to assess the level of achievement with relative accuracy with regard to the objectives stated for each module.

This paper investigates the middle area between an extreme modular and an extreme linear approach and considers the difference between a modular system restricted by educational, professional and administrative needs and a linear system softened by the choice of options. It goes on to indicate a method of distinguishing between the two, however complex the circumstances, by the test of one's ability to automatically discuss the student's previous route. It comes down in favour of modularity for a teacher training institution of modest size which needs to diversify. Assessment procedures are also investigated and, although both linear and modular systems have their own implications for assessment, it is necessary to resist these and seek a varied solution on educational grounds and student needs. A modular system again has the edge here because of the existence of relatively precise objectives for each module which can be assessed with some degree of efficiency. The debate between modular and linear courses is really a non-argument as pure examples do not exist. Educationally it has been shown that advantages exist in both and we need to learn these so that they can be incorporated in our course planning.

# Discussion Papers

The three articles in this section were written by the principals of three of the colleges of education that have been attempting to come to terms with the changing situation in teacher education. They were asked if they would write short articles which identified the major issues as they saw them, and which would be sources for discussion during the three days of the conference.

William Percival, Principal of Charlotte Mason College of Education, Ambleside, has taken as his theme the 'challenge of change' and looks back to the original objectives of the movement for change in teacher education. He shows that what should have been an educational debate turned into 'local politicing and fight for status, power and authority'. It has not, he regrets, arisen from our responsibility to the children and the generation of teachers to teach them.

Norman Evans, Principal of Bishop Lonsdale College of Education, Derby, turns his attention to the search for a new identity for teacher educators. He suggests three areas where boundaries need to be defined or re-defined. The first is the nature of the professional partnership between teachers in schools and teachers in colleges. A second area is the area of professional courses where he argues the colleges were most criticised and the criticism most just. Thirdly, he looks at the academic organisation and considers how the tutors need to relate to their academic peers. Through re-defining these areas, he argues, teacher educators may find their new identity.

Bernard Fisher, Principal of the City of Leicester College of Education, in his article debates the problems of consecutive versus concurrent education courses and points sharply to some damaging defects of consecutive courses upon the quality of professional courses. He also explores the unintended results of the presently proposed distribution of teaching places and institutions, and looks at the problems of training for a rapidly changing school system which cannot be overcome, he argues, with consecutive training, nor an all-graduate teaching profession ill-prepared for the job awaiting them in the schools.

# The challenge of change

William Percival

When I received the invitation to attend the Brighton Conference on Changing Patterns in Teacher Education in April 1975 my heart sank at the prospect of another of those recently all-too-frequent, and sad, interminable sessions, when those of us in teacher training met to wallow in a sea of self-pity and mutual commiseration, to accuse our masters in Elizabeth House of malevolently destroying a long-cherished system, to accuse the James Committee of prejudice, our professional association of betrayal, the polytechnics of territorial ambitions and the universities of callous indifference.  At the present time the battlefield is covered in smoke as we dart from shell hole to shell hole seeking either a group to join (university, polytechnic or friendly college of further education) or to remain alone in our hole in the ground.  When we find a lull we spend countless hours and expend reams of paper designing new degree and diploma courses which no-one wants but which we believe we could mount and which might ensure survival till the war ends.  Just as we think the guns are quieter a new offensive breaks out; increasing numbers of sixth formers do not want higher education and the country cannot afford more of it.  Then comes the final blow: the population figures upon which the White Paper and Circular 7/73 were based were widely optimistic. More of us must be lost; the plans on which we drew up our battle lines were based on false intelligence.  Anyway, the battle now seems to be about something quite different; it is about organisation, structures, money, survival.

But this is not how we started - the James and the previous enquiries were set up because many teachers, students, LEAs and some staff in colleges were utterly dissatisfied with what was provided as teacher training. The evidence was wide-spread and was clear. It is depressing to realise that the cause of all this discontent still remains, and in four years precious little has been done to solve it. James asked for a debate about principles. Instead, we have all been busy taking up defensive positions and digging our trenches. No-one emerged from the post-James debate with credit; the universities on the whole had failed to bring anything substantial of quality or any new sense of direction to teacher training which did not have, and still does not have, any substantial position in their institutions; the teachers failed to see the great opportunity offered to them by the James' emphasis on Cycle III; and the colleges were distracted by the reports of minor but sillier organisational proposals. Disappointingly the publication of the James Report was followed by no national debate about the principles, design and practice of teacher training. Then, in publishing the White Paper and Circular 7/73, the DES made sure that any discussions from thenceforth would be about everything but educational principles and practice! For the next two years our energies have been devoted to abuse of the DES, to discussion about projection figures, and to local politicking and the fight for status, power and authority. Of course, in defence of these battle-worn, bemused and leaderless troops one can argue that the scale of the external factors - a turning away from higher education, a drop in the birth-rate, and a desperate economic crisis - is too great to allow for any rational debate, and that a patchwork organisational solution is all we can expect to see for the next few years. That is not good enough. Alec Ross (THES, 14th February 1975) is right; our first responsibility is to the children and to the generation of teachers who will teach them. I fear that we have had no national debate, not because we were too busy trying to save our institutions in the form we had known them, but because we were too isolated and complacent to appreciate the criticisms levelled at us, and too timid to go back and start again from a close study of needs and objectives.

In looking to the future my hope is that we shall look again at the James Report, at the evidence submitted to it, and take note of the deep groundswell of dis-satisfaction which gave rise to it. Then we should seek to explore how the first tentative steps might be taken to begin an analysis of needs in teacher training. We must make a sustained attempt to look at what was wrong and think out a programme for educational and not just institutional change. Many local authorities and teachers made the mistake in the days of comprehensive re-organisation in the sixties of assuming that new designations and new organisations automatically implied new philosophies, objectives, values and methods, but new 'comprehensives' could mean old 'grammar' or 'secondary modern' writ large. Teacher training in a polytechnic or a new college of higher education can be just as irrelevant and arid as it was in the former college of education.

James pointed to some serious short-comings; the failure to provide training for the challenges then in schools (the open-plan primary, the mixed-ability class in the comprehensive school); to the gulf between theory and practice and to theory which appeared to have no relevance; to the conservative influence of the universities; and to the unanimous dis-satisfaction with post-graduate training.

There are a number of important questions which now need to be asked. What is the meaning of professionalism in terms of teaching today and how are expectations and assumptions changing; on the part of government and public in the post-Houghton days, on the part of teachers beginning to accept the concept of a right to opportunities for further professional development and qualifications; by teacher educators who can now plan initially for teacher training as merely the first phase of induction to a profession; and by teachers who might increasingly be torn between 'professional' aspirations and a growing belief in 'unionism'?

Having looked closely at the needs of the teacher about to take up his first post, there will then be a paramount need to examine how this can be met in the light of the organisational patterns now developing. Can there be well-designed consecutive type courses in which the first one or two years have sufficient general and non-professional substance still to leave the student the choice of teaching or other career, without distorting the content or direction of the course? Can the concept of a professional centre for initial and in-service education for teachers with its essential need for close links with teachers and schools (and possibly joint staffing with schools) thrive in a huge institution such as a polytechnic in which teacher training is inevitably a minor segment? All teacher training units are going to be small; can they, or should they, offer wide choice within their walls?

Above all, we need to examine what are the factors which allow a teacher training college, or indeed any institute of higher education, to ascertain need and if required produce rational changes. At the time of writing I only know of one or two teacher training institutions which have used the opportunities given by James and the White Paper to start again from the beginning and develop totally new courses. At Charlotte Mason College, a small college threatened even before the White Paper with the possibility of closure, the Academic Board decided that boldness was the best line of defence. Encouraged by a DES-supported and financed project at the College to develop a course which substituted for main academic subjects a range of courses in applications of the primary school curriculum, they set up an enquiry into the needs of the new teacher. From there, using curriculum development techniques, a new type of degree course in Applied Education was developed, to be validated at the levels of Diploma of Higher Education, B. Ed Ordinary and B. Ed Honours by the University of Lancaster, the first new style B. Ed degrees to be so approved by any university. The Academic Board then proceeded to design and establish a completely new staffing structure which required all staff to accept the ending of posts then held and apply for new posts. It then instituted an extensive and thorough comprehensive staff development programme and restructured the constitution and composition of its Academic Board.

This is perhaps a modest enough achievement and one which is much easier in an institution which is small and likely to remain independent and monotechnic. However, it could also be argued that change could be developed on a much greater scale in a larger institution given the same willingness to accept the need to consider radical alternatives. Timidity, complacency and obsession with organisational change alone will get us nowhere. Unless we provide courses which meet the criticisms of the sixties we shall betray the teachers and the children of the eighties and the nineties.

# Searching for a new identity

**Norman Evans**

Many teacher educators now feel orphaned. The ensured flow of students into training and thence as teachers into schools, and the assured vocational context for their work have gone. The father and mother of security are dead. And as any orphaned adolescent finds, the experience of searching for a new identity is painful. Teacher education is supposed to be growing to maturity through joining the family of higher education. The White Paper 'Education, a Framework for Expansion' identified 'the wholehearted acceptance of the colleges of education into the family of higher education institutions' as one of the six objectives of the James Committee which received wide support and are 'fully accepted by the Government'. The search is in deadly earnest. But there are problems.

First of all there is the problem of learning to live with disappointed hopes and the anxious fears which succeed them. At first, the re-organisation of the colleges seemed to promise rich possibilities through a delayed commitment to teaching, diversification of courses, greater choice for students. Temporarily at any rate there is not much in prospect. Emphasis on nursery education, doubts about the number of teachers who can be employed, sharp reductions in the number of teacher education places, are all pressing applicants to committing themselves at entry to teaching. Diversification of courses looks an extremely doubtful development against the evidence of reduced numbers of applications for higher education. And if the numbers of students in training are smaller, then inevitably the range of choice of courses open to them is restricted. As a result of all this, it is clear that not so many tutors from colleges of education can be employed. The merger is the prescribed remedy. But mergers mean unsuspected quantities of lower level work in new kinds of colleges where former college of education tutors may have only a limited say. Fear can turn to nightmare.

But in the cool morning light the changing patterns have to be recognised, the search for identity has to begin. It can only begin within boundaries which are both recognised and accepted. Three such boundaries could be a professional partnership of teachers in schools and teachers in colleges for training teachers; the professional courses which replace the former curriculum courses; and academic organisation. The definition of each boundary could constitute a highly significant change.

First the training partnership. The need is clear. A strong case can be made for claiming that if in the heyday of the fifties and sixties expansion period colleges had forged a secure working partnership with schools for the training of teachers, the progression of events from the NUT campaign over the teaching of reading, via the Select Committee of the House of Commons, the Edward Short Inquiry into Area Training Organisation, the Tory Manifesto of 1970, the James Committee, to the White Paper and Circular 7/73, could not have been written. But now the Regional Co-ordinating Committees which are to replace the Area Training Organisations, the Induction Year or whatever becomes of it, and In-service provision, all voice a professional need for a close partnership as a matter of principle. The same need is of paramount importance as a matter of pragmatic practice. With central and local Government so hard pressed to make the money go round, to a very large extent the success of both the in-service provision and development of an induction year must depend on harnessing all the available resources to common ends. Moreover, unless there is careful co-operation with LEAs, schools and teachers, colleges' potential contributions may be ignored or spurned or just not sought. To put it in another way, the gulf between the training system and the teaching system must be closed.

This points to a deeper professional significance. One of the really serious weaknesses in the otherwise strong reply the colleges have made to the accusation that within their courses theory and practice stay unrelated, is that as a matter of fact too many students get caught uncomfortably when colleges say one thing and schools say another. The James Committee (3.7) made some of its most severe comments for school practice. 'Many students are vehement in asserting that teaching practice is one of the most valuable and one of the worst conducted parts of their training. Many teachers in school remain in ignorance of the purpose of teaching practice, and, even more important, of the contribution to it expected of them. . . . The result is sometimes that students may receive little detailed professional guidance'.

Where that is a literal description, clearly things are disgraceful. Frequently the problems seem to lie in interpretation rather than ignorance. Generally where it is a difference of interpretation, then the difference may be real but more apparent than real, and not fundamental. Usually with careful examination differences can be resolved. It is true they can perpetuate misunderstandings and misconceptions which schools and colleges may have of one another. They can be personally wounding to tutors and even baffling professionally. But that is not their real significance. These differences between schools and colleges prevent students from benefiting as much as they should from the knowledge, experience and expertise of teachers in schools and tutors in colleges. Differences which place students in this position are anti-educational and strictly unprofessional. The surest way of dealing with this - though not necessarily of removing difficulties, exploring them can be a highly effective educational vehicle - and so improving the preparation of teachers is to associate teachers in schools with teachers in colleges, with the teacher education course. This implies looking beyond the question of who does what on school practice, though that is a necessary step forward, to the selection, the tutoring and the assessment of students. Some colleges have moved part or all the way towards this partnership which postulates not only shared contributions but shared responsibilities.

Wherever this is so a potent in-service programme is tacitly followed. But not all colleges have managed it. This boundary will only be secure when this partnership is established as part of the structure of professional practice and of the teacher education system.

One of the gains to teacher educationalists from the present confusion is that tutors are exercising greater control than before over the courses they are going to teach. Whatever the constraints imposed by universities or CNAA as validators, with the experience of the B. Ed behind them, tutors have only themselves to blame if the courses they are going to teach are not substantially what they want. It follows that they have substantial power to set the professional partnership firmly within the design of courses.

This enlarged control of the college curriculum, which amounts to a considerable change of pattern in itself, has a significance for the second suggested boundary; professional courses. Generally speaking curriculum courses in the certificate and present B. Ed satisfied no-one. It is rather like the complaints made by graduates about the Post-graduate Certificate of Education. After studying courses with some intensity and application in education and main course, curriculum courses failed to satisfy because they were not always sufficiently demanding, frequently less coherently thought and taught than other parts of the course, and it has to be said, treated sometimes casually by tutors as well as students. The context for that state of affairs is vital; to all intents and purposes curriculum courses were not validated. This state of affairs is changing abruptly. As part of a degree programme professional courses are being validated along with every other part of the student's course, and of all the tasks set for course designers this is the most demanding of all.

In Teacher Education and Training (3.2 - 3.5) the James Committee made great play with what they took to be the inadequacies of the concurrent pattern of training. If teacher educators really believe that personal education and professional preparation can proceed simultaneously with a three or four year course, now they have the opportunity to prove it. If the balance in the old courses between main subject, education, professional courses and school practice has proved inadequate where each had more or less a third of the time available, then the balance can be changed. If there is a gap between the study of the theory of education and classroom practice as mediated through professional courses, then there is every opportunity to bring the two into closer association as part of a newly validated degree. If there are serious objections to having the same kind of course programme for a student intending to teach in a nursery school as for someone hoping to teach in a middle school or as a specialist in a secondary school, then new courses can offer every opportunity to establish differing programmes for differing kinds of teaching. A residual problem remains that in this country an employing authority is able to appoint any qualified teacher to any post, but that raises a different range of questions. As far as the design of new courses for teacher education is concerned, the pivot is the professional course. And it is an essential boundary to secure.

Trying to define this boundary is in one sense to extend the argument of professional partnership. Courses designed to develop the professional skills of a teacher over a wide range of the curriculum will always face the problem of attempting simultaneously to educate the student, giving him a firm grasp of knowledge and enabling him to use it through his teaching. But they cannot possibly be successful without the children. And children are in schools. So at the very least a kind of close co-operation with teachers is necessary. But more than that, professional courses which do win validation as an integral part of a B.Ed will transform the nature of the course. Firm academic foundations must be laid through gathering appropriate material from the contributory disciplines to the study of education so that those parts of the course which may deal for example with the teaching of reading or the teaching of mathematics can be set within a coherent academic structure of theory and practice of education. As that happens another boundary will be secured.

The third boundary is academic organisation. There are many facets to this. There is the way in which tutors are organised to contribute to differing parts of the course; education and main subjects and professional courses, or however these elements appear in the new style B. Eds. There is the way the students' work is organised as between lectures, class contact time, tutorials, school experience (and perhaps other practical experience) and private study. There is the way tutors of courses are going to relate to one another and to the validators of their new courses, which will require a new kind of academic organisation. This will be true for the surviving 'monotechnics'. But there is another kind of academic organisation which is going to affect most teacher educators; their relationships with a new multipurpose institution. In some ways this is the most difficult boundary to plot because of anxieties about teacher education being downgraded as a minority interest and the consequent uncertainty about how to set about exploiting the academic organisation of the college to secure necessary resources. But in one way this boundary described as academic organisation is the easiest to plot. Tutors from the colleges have to recognise what they have to contribute to the new colleges and to set about contributing it vigorously.

With all its imperfections, the teaching style developed by the colleges can give an excellent service to higher education students in the second flight. This style has twin supports. At institutional level the courses have been a corporate responsibility of the entire tutorial body. The advances in academic self-government achieved by the colleges of education as a result of the Weaver Report set them striding into the 'family of higher education' in the way in which they transacted their academic business, long before the current debate began about which family they belonged to. At personal level tutors have accepted (to excess sometimes) a direct responsibility for the progress of their students which has been exercised through the tutorial system, rooted in a residential tradition. A simple comparison between the numbers of tutors in any college of education who have their own studies, and the numbers of staff in the nearest polytechnic or college of advanced further education makes the point. Each of these strands is in some way envied by many thoughtful further education lecturers as they in their turn consider the institutional changes which are affecting their colleges. With perception, tact, proper humility and energy, tutors who value the way they have done things in the past can easily find a warmer reception for their ideas than they might anticipate. They should not underestimate the significance of the contribution they can make to the teaching of courses outside teacher education programmes. Nor should they underestimate their power to affect the new colleges of which they become part.

These three boundaries of professional partnership, of professional courses, and academic organisation can be taken to describe the area within which teacher education will continue. As each boundary is staked out, morale can rise. A professional partnership can undoubtedly produce a far greater sense of professional security. Professional courses can correct an academic weakness in a course. And through academic re-organisation a wider sense of purpose for teacher educators can develop. Within these boundaries a new identity can grow. Professional acceptance can be won through professional validation of the professional preparation of teachers for their responsibilities in schools. And if it should happen that the pre-service courses become more effective than their predecessors then the morale of teacher education could be sustained at a higher level than before. The search for a new identity will be over.

# Four major issues

**Bernard Fisher**

Colleges have undergone a traumatic experience during the last three years, the effects of which are only just beginning to wear off. Pounded by their critics in the James Report, urged by the White Paper, government circulars and 'authorities' to reconstitute their courses and slough off their alleged isolation in monotechnic institutions, faced with simultaneous demands to build in Dip. H. E. courses, vocational programmes orientated to non-teaching careers, to re-think the whole philosophy of teacher education[1] and to contract the number of their students while retaining and even expanding all the options open to them, the colleges, not surprisingly, find themselves contemplating somewhat ruefully the ruins of their former achievements, fearful of what the future portends for the quality of the new entrants into the profession.

Emerging new patterns of organisation of the colleges have brought in their train a host of challenges and problems. Among the major issues with which teacher education is confronted, the whole question of course structures must inevitably loom large. The challenge presented to the concept of concurrent training is not new. Arguments of disruption of academic studies caused by the need to weld practical experience on to theoretical studies, resulting in superficial or broken courses, of the need to train non-teacher training students alongside the normal entry without such deterrents to continuous study have not calmed very real fears that the consecutive course will keep motivated teachers away from the very experience which brought them to college, turn the first two years of their course into a mere extension of their sixth form studies, and put them at a very real disadvantage with concurrent course students both in terms of their professional training and the inroads made into the academic demands of the fourth year of an Honours Degree by the intercalation of a year of professional orientation between the second and fourth years of their course. That there will be a diminution in the amount of time available for practical experience is almost a foregone conclusion. In the face of a vast volume of opinion from the schools, the Unions and the students themselves[2] that teachers in training need more, and longer, periods in schools, the consecutive course bids fair to bring in its train those very features of the James programme of 'cycles' with its four weeks in schools which caused such an outcry at the time of the publication of the Report.

A corollary of this problem is the very emphasis now being placed on academic qualifications and study. Without denying the value, indeed the need of a strong academic background, statistics show[3] that the number of two A level entry candidates to higher education is unlikely to fill the places available, and that unless a huge self-defeating system of 'special admission' procedures is adopted and in this way allowed to attenuate the entry, there will be wholesale defections from applicants for teaching. 'There would not in the short term be enough applicants with the (two A level) qualification to meet all teacher supply needs, and a policy of wholesale exemptions would undermine the standing of the new degree.'[4] The purpose of creating the high level entry, which was at least plausible while it was believed that the number of entrants to higher education was growing at the same time as the demand for teachers was diminishing was to create a recruitment area for the new Dip. H. E. and a flexibility which James, the White Paper and Circular 7/73 deemed to be imperative to provide that wide range of courses and freedom of transfer into and out of teaching. 'The Government have sympathy with the sincere desire on the part of a growing number of students to be given more help in acquiring - and discovering how to apply - knowledge and skills related more directly to the decisions which will face them in their careers . . . system of units and credits . . . to ease transfer from one course or institution to another.'[5] Once more these proposals have been overtaken by events, and the slowdown in the demand for higher education creates a new situation which renders nugatory the major premise on which the consecutive course was constructed. Doubts are even being cast upon the availability of the new diversified courses for which these consecutive patterns were advocated after the polytechnics have pre-empted on almost every area of study and training which might have provided the alternatives with which to fill the vacant teacher-training places in the colleges and thereby ensured the viability of the institution and the future of existing staffs. There seems little doubt that the whole corpus of teacher education is undergoing radical surgery - it will be for the schools to consider whether the quality of our products has been enhanced by these new methods, which, if we are honest, are little more than the old and often criticised system of training as practised within the UDEs, with the added handicap of only two years of academic study before the professional year of the PGCE, now to be equated with the third year of the college course. Proponents can with justice point to the introduction of the study of the major disciplines of education into the modular structure of the first two years and the practical experience which is to form part of that course. It will do little to calm the fears of students and schools that these periods must be at the expense of real practical school experience and ironically of the amount of time available for the study of their academic courses for which the whole consecutive pattern was developed. 'Consultations have indicated that there is now greater support for concurrent courses for those wishing to commit themselves to teaching at an early stage than there appeared to be when the (James) Committee were engaged in their task.'[6]

Of equal importance to the profession are the consequences of the declared policy of the DES drastically to reduce the number of teacher-training students in the new large amalgamated institutions in order to make possible the survival of the smaller colleges. It is clear that there the DES was presented with the cruel dilemma of having to choose between the closure of a number of smaller colleges or a reduction in the entry to the larger institutions if numbers were to be brought down to their acceptable minimum. Faced with the very natural outcry of the small colleges (properly supported by their professional association) the DES bowed to the inevitable and accepted the need to keep most of the colleges open. But that decision of itself is fraught with dangers to the quality both of entrants to the profession and the training that will be available to them. The large institutions are normally situated in areas where mergers are easy to achieve, tend to attract the top calibre students, and by their size are able to offer many more courses and qualifications. If then students are to be turned away from such institutions by a restriction in their entry numbers in order to keep alive the smaller colleges, it is clear that many will reconsider their previous intention to apply for teacher-training. The smaller colleges by their very nature are likely to be unable to offer that width of options and that depth of study which students will be seeking, nor can they diversify in the way proposed by the White Paper and everyone else, as an essential element in transferability and delay in choice of careers. 'The recommendations we have already made . . . for dropping the requirement that entrants should be committed to a teaching career demand a flexible overall course structure within which colleges could cater for a variety of student needs and interests.'[7] The James Report when it was published spoke in similar vein. 'The colleges would no longer be training teachers in isolation.'[8] While the THES in a leading article on 24th January 1975 clearly came to the same conclusion.[9]

Finally, the spread of the belief, however laudable, in an all-graduate profession will further dissuade applications from many who in the past have made invaluable contributions to teaching without claiming to be of university calibre in their academic potential. It may be that the solution to this problem will lie in the development of a truly professional degree, as many claim, but it is difficult to avoid the conclusion that such a qualification, if it is to have credibility, will need to have built into it the same intellectual demands in the theoretical study of education as are at present required in traditional degree structures. The issues then that face the world of teacher education may well result in the creation of a tripartite system within its ranks. There will be in the first case the traditional offering of the university, the graduate with his PGCE. In the second place will come the large institutions, their numbers reduced to the smallest viable minimum, with students having access to a long list of courses, careers and qualifications, but with the built-in danger that the very diversity of offerings might lead to their professional training being subordinated to the demands made upon their courses by the requirements of the Dip. H. E. the resulting consecutive structure and the need to remain flexible in career opportunities throughout the first two years of the course. The advantage which would accrue would clearly be that wide variety of courses, provided that the resulting modular structure did not create a lack of coherence and patchwork quilt qualifications, to prevent which much counselling and overall supervision will have to be built into the whole course.

The third leg of the triad, to use the vocabulary of pre-Spens days, would be the students of the small, largely monotechnic colleges with their restricted offerings, little chance of graduate qualifications or alternative courses, but retaining that special ethos of a college of education which many of us have come to recognise and to value in its personal relationships and close-knit community spirit which in these days of monolithic impersonal structures should not go unrecognised.

Are we about to create in the realm of teacher-training that situation in which the schools found themselves at the time of the Endowed Schools Commission, the Spens report and the system of tripartitism which after the 1944 Act evoked such an outburst against the transparent disparity of three parts of a system whose author inveighed against any suggestion that it need result in inequality? Will what we are now about to do redound to the credit of the training agencies and the advantage of the schools?

Any consideration of the changing pattern of teacher education cannot fail to take account of the many and varied patterns now existing within the schools themselves. Until the fairly recent past, the conditions with which a young entrant to the profession would be confronted in whatever school to which he was appointed were almost entirely predictable. Whether it was the tripartite system in operation or the developing comprehensive re-organisation there were but few variants on the general theme embodied within primary and secondary education. True it was that a number of authorities were experimenting with middle schools, a few still retained the once popular bilateral and 'other secondary' systems until their virtual demise after the publication of circular 10/67; Leicestershire had its own almost unique Upper and High School Plan and so on, but there was little to distinguish the pattern of education within the schools themselves. A few daring heads and their staffs experimented with early versions of curriculum reform and classroom organisation, but generally it was possible to assert with a reasonable degree of confidence that colleges could prepare students for the operational and educational conditions they were likely to encounter not only in their teaching practices but also in the schools to which they would be appointed on the successful completion of their courses.

Today the scene is vastly different. To all the variants of transfer at 8 - 12; 9 - 13; 11 - 14; 11 - 16; 11 - 18 and Sixth Form Colleges have been added the integrated day, the integrated timetable, team teaching, the open classroom, the open-plan school, mixed ability grouping, interdisciplinary studies, family grouping, contract, project and machine teaching, i.t.a., new maths and the like, all of which need careful study and understanding if a student or new member of staff is to fit harmoniously and efficiently into the pattern of these different conditions. Careful planning by the college can adapt the student's school experience to the type most suited to his own predilections and abilities, but it cannot shield him from the circumstances of change within the school to which he is eventually appointed or to differing conditions in other parts of the country. Nor can it give him a sound basis on which to judge and evaluate these new approaches. Experience has shown that unless students obtain the widest possible experience in varying types of schools difficulties can arise at a later stage in their career. Nor can this experience be gained by odd half days spent in the environment of so close a society as the modern school.

And so we return to our theme that it would seem an urgent precondition for the production of well-trained students that their courses should contain many and varied experiences spread over the whole period of their studies. Yet this is in direct conflict with the very essence of the emerging patterns of teacher education, with their accent on two years of consecutive academic study, with virtually the whole of their professional education constricted within the limits of the third year of the course. It is of course true that some colleges are requiring students who display an interest in a career in teaching to undertake studies of the academic disciplines of education - philosophy, psychology, sociology and history - during the first two years and are planning to include school 'visits' within the limits set by the time available to these educational studies, but there must be cause for concern that spasmodic and superficial experiences of this nature can ever replace the longer continuous periods of school practices that are necessary really to acclimatise students to the society of the school and to bring real understanding of the changed circumstances in which education takes place in our modern society. The author has bitter memories of his own students plunged into a school environment so alien to everything previously experienced that the practice was doomed to failure from the first, and the student sometimes disenchanted forever from the prospect of embracing the career so freely chosen on his admission to college. And the inevitable conclusion to be drawn is that the greater the requirement to involve students in study and school experience of this type during the first two years the less flexible becomes the consecutive course planned in the first instance round a Dip. H. E. specifically to permit students to keep open their choice of career until a later stage of their Higher Education studies. It seems incontrovertible that the changing patterns within the schools themselves will force upon the colleges a reconsideration of the content and educational processes of their programmes. It may well be concluded that their constriction within the Procrustean bed of the Dip. H. E. has brought in its train more difficulties than advantages, without even producing the flexibility that was intended (except perhaps the freedom to opt out of teaching!) and could even be the cause of an increasing number of first class highly motivated students withdrawing from a profession to which they felt themselves so clearly committed before their courses began. It is in this context that the small three year concurrent course monotechnics may have a significant role to play, but one that will bring the whole process by which we train our teachers back full circle to many of the conditions that prevailed in the years before 1960 and against which James, the White Paper, and numerous critics railed so loudly before publication of the Robbins Report in 1963 and the ATOs enquiry into teacher training in 1969.

It is then the changing role of the teacher in the re-organised school and classroom that demands more and more emphasis on longer and more frequent periods of observation and participation on the part of our students. Yet these very possibilities are at risk in the new emphasis on academic qualifications, consecutive training with its two years of 'rigorous academic study' looking into a Dip. H. E. that no teacher will ever want or obtain and with the consequential reduction in the number and length of teaching practices. There must be some concern about proposals emanating from Departments of Education and educational theorists that these can adequately be replaced by the weekly visit or the occasional week or two likely to be available in the new pattern of courses.

But time is pressing, decisions are being taken without due time for research and consultation, and as we rush headlong into the Brave New World of teacher preparation we may well reflect that evolution takes a little longer than revolution but is usually found to be more effective in adapting to the needs of society at each stage of our history.

In this article I have attempted to identify four major issues and two likely consequences which seem to me to demand immediate and serious consideration; viz, the impact of the change to consecutive courses on the quality of our professional training, the effect of demanding two A level qualifications for admission to such courses, the likely results of the proposed drastic reduction in teacher training numbers in merged institutions in order to keep alive the majority of the smaller colleges, and the possible effect on entry to teacher training of a move towards an all-graduate profession. The consequences of these reforms, it is suggested, may result in the development of a tripartite system of teacher training and inadequate practical experience to meet the needs of the re-organised schools.

REFERENCES

1. 'At this conference (NAHT) . . . the delegates passed by 428 votes to 2 a motion demanding an immediate investigation into the teaching methods of colleges of education.' Why Tommy isn't learning, S Froome, 1970

2. 'The Plowden Report agrees with the students that colleges should have more contact with the schools.' S Froome, ibid, p 138

3. 'Last year only forty per cent of the students accepted had obtained two A levels.' Central Register and Clearing House, January 1975

4. 'Education, A Framework for Expansion', page 22, paragraph 79

5. Ibid, page 31, paragraph 108

6. Ibid, page 21, paragraph 74

7. 'The Professional Education of Teachers', ATCDE Memorandum to the James Committee, page 4, paragraph 3.1

8. Teacher Education and Training, page 69, paragraph 6.8

9. THES, 24th January 1975: 'The effect of the colleges returning to teacher-training units of between 350 and 600 will be fewer innovations, less options for students, more isolated training units, and little room for improvements in the quality of teacher training. A better course might be for the selective closure of a few more colleges so that a large proportion of teaching training courses can be concentrated in large diversified institutions.'

# Conclusions

In this final section we begin to look more specifically to the future. A feature of the conference were the discussion groups where there was a series of analyses of the major issues. There appeared to be two major areas of debate; the first curriculum issues relating to the form of the B. Ed in the future and secondly the institutional position of teacher education after the present round of mergers. The interesting point which appeared rightly to exercise the minds of many people was the likely effect on teacher education of the move from its central position in a monotechnic to that of only one of many competing areas in the new structures. Education faculties might be disadvantaged by their late arrival in the larger institutions. A point on which there was unanimous agreement was that there would be a need in the future to see teacher education more clearly as a distinctive area and the formation of a learned association to cover its academic interests was urged.

Roger Webster in his article covers many issues but one which seems especially relevant is his concern that the present crisis should be seized as an opportunity for far reaching curriculum innovation. The form he suggests should be inexorably linked to educational practice and this, he suggests, has two implications. First education must become an integrated study and secondly is that if one is to be concerned with the analysis of practice it must be based on practical work - which in turn leads to the need for institutional integration and improved relationships with the schools.

In the third paper, this point is taken up in a consideration of the conclusions the editors were able to draw from a study of the previous articles and also some positive points of view of their own. It was felt that two particular areas of teacher education needed analysis. Firstly the curiously muted response to the opportunity to rewrite the courses. The blank cheque offered has been viewed with suspicion and the chance has not yet been seized as eagerly as many would have hoped. Why is this? It is suggested an organisational analysis shows how the colleges' decision-making structure has been dislocated by the crisis, making response difficult. The second major facet of the problem, it is argued, derives from insufficient attention to the actual felt needs of the new teacher in the school. Using results of research carried out at Brighton, it is argued that there needs to be a greater dissolution of the boundaries between the colleges and schools.

Finally, let us hope these conference papers will lead others to carry on this important debate in spite of the continuing demands on the time of those most able to contribute. As we argue in the final paper, in education at the moment to stand still is to fall behind. In this context this means we need to nurture our 'futurologists' for few are likely to be able to raise their heads to take the longer view.

# The Major issues:
# a summary of discussion reports

M St J Raggett and M W Clarkson

The Conference had as one of its main objectives that of acting as a national forum for discussion between those most concerned with curriculum development in this area. To implement this objective discussion groups were set up and the proceedings recorded. This brief account of some of the major issues raised is derived from the conclusions of the five groups. The issues can be seen to divide into two areas first, there is the curriculum development area concerned with the form of the B. Ed in the future, and the second is concerned with the institutional position of teacher education after the present changes have taken place.

The curriculum problems, it was suggested, were complex. First was the problem of entry as many argued the two A level criterion was inflexible and probably unjustified and harmful. For example there were those who failed A levels because of poor sixth form teaching or who were just late developers. It was also an inappropriate condition for particular categories of students such as those seeking entry to courses of study in the expressive and performing arts. There was a need to find new criteria for selection and to convince the CNAA etc of their validity. Second, was the problem of concurrent versus consecutive forms of B. Ed - should 'school experience' and 'teacher training' occur parallel or following the part of the course less directly related to teaching? One group argued strongly in favour of concurrence whilst recognising the problems of transfer from parallel courses. In reaching this view the group was mindful of the following factors:

a) the need for students to have early experience of the life and work of schools, and meaningful contact with children over a substantial period of time;
b) the value of distributed rather than massed practice, which allows periods for consolidation and critical evaluation;
c) the move towards concurrence in the training of other professional groups (for example, medicine, architecture and engineering).

A third issue was the nature of the professional element in the B. Ed courses. Whilst there appeared to be consensus on the need to make the professional course the central feature of the B. Ed certain points emerged from the discussion:

a) professional courses need to be directly and positively related to success in the classroom and to be intellectually challenging. It was felt that the courses should help the student to approach practical problems with a depth of understanding placing the problems in appropriate contexts and bringing relevant theoretical concepts and procedures to bear. Thus work on the teaching of geography, for example, should involve study of the nature of the subject and of the development of children's thinking in relation to geography in particular. The vital ability to control pupils which the student must develop arises from his being able to plan flexibly and realistically and to review and modify effectively the action taken, in the light of experience.
b) research undertaken by staff teaching B. Ed courses should be largely in the professional area so as to add to the knowledge of the application of educational theory to teaching problems. It should further the development of theoretical analysis by springing directly from teaching (such as that of interaction in the classroom), and help to link colleges and schools. It was thought that group research projects undertaken by staff, perhaps assisted by students, will have more value than small-scale pieces of individual research.
c) education studies (that is, sociology, psychology and philosophy

of education, etc) have an important function in supporting
professional studies, although this is not to say that this is
their only function. It was felt to be important for students
to get to grips with one or two of the theoretical studies of
education, for without this they are unlikely to gain qualified
teacher status, independence of mind or ability to emancipate
themselves from the 'common-sense' view of an area of
practical problems in a manner which is needed for a professional;

d) professional courses should be concerned with specific age-
ranges of pupils, but this should be a matter of emphasis rather
than a set of mutually exclusive concerns. It is perhaps para-
doxically important for the student to be able to focus his
attention on an age-range (and a couple of subjects in the case
of secondary students) if he is to learn to think freely and
flexibly about educational problems.

The second major area of concern was with regard to the position of
teacher educators and teacher education in the new institutions. There were
seen to be at least two important problems; what would be the position of
teacher education in larger institutions and what was the best use for
resources released by the decrease in initial teacher training. As to the
first problem, many believed that the polytechnic as opposed to monotechnic might not be as healthy for teacher training as this would now be a
minority activity. Re-organisation might for example leave teacher
education in polytechnics in competition with prestigious schools or
faculties, for example, accountancy with its high earning power. Moreover, the teacher educators themselves whether in universities or polytechnics might be dispersed into existing departments so losing the
coherence familiar in the monotechnic institution. As to the second point,
it was clear that many believe the human resources represented by the
tutors needed to be utilised to the full in the new situation by involvement
in new areas. Diversification of courses and especially those leading
to B A degrees were seen to be useful but fears were expressed about
attracting students in sufficient numbers.

In-service training of teachers was felt to be another important area which could be expanded. It was suggested for example that teachers could be released for courses while student teachers were undertaking teaching practices in schools. It was also suggested that some lecturers could undertake part-time teaching in schools, thus releasing extra teachers for in-service education without adding to the financial burden for the local authorities to any great extent. The idea of a college of education as a community college was mooted; providing continuing education to those who needed it in the locality. It was stated that not all persons wanted an Open University method of obtaining a degree but that part-time courses in college leading to a degree or other worthwhile qualifications could meet needs in the community. It could also provide other courses of an extra-mural nature for those interested. However, it was realised that the economic climate is not favourable at present for expansion of adult education.

Finally it was clear many agreed that teacher education was sufficiently distinctive to support a learned association of its own. The area now needed to develop a professional structure relevant to its new position in the community of higher and further education and to support the slimmer but hopefully more effective teacher education in the post re-organisation situation.

# The future of teacher training

**Roger Webster**

Some years ago, Sir Gordon Russell gave a lecture in Cardiff on contemporary furniture design. He must, I think, have been a little taken aback when, at the end of his talk, one of the audience commented that it was easy enough to design modern furniture. What he wanted to know was, How could the design of antiques be improved?

In reforming the curriculum and organisation of educational institutions we are trying to do just that: to improve the design of antiques. Sometimes we just add a coat of varnish (give an old course a new name or produce a glossier prospectus), or we tack on a decorative knob or two, in secondary schools a ROSLA knob, in colleges of education a professional studies knob or a fourth year B. Ed knob. If a section of the antique is thoroughly infested with worm, it may have to be replaced with new wood (or possibly a piece of simulated plastic, as when Greek and Latin become classical studies). Sometimes the antique, for reasons you might think to be quite philistine, may be taken apart, bits added and an entirely new piece created. Or, in the last resort, the wood itself may be planed down and used for an entirely new piece of furniture.

I have developed this rather tortuous metaphor to emphasise that curriculum reform never begins de novo. We are always altering an existing situation; it is impossible to create an entirely new curriculum. My metaphor also draws attention to the distinction between different degrees of curriculum change, and points to the difficulty of bringing about radical change. It is a brave man who would tear apart even the most creaking piece of Chippendale. It takes an even braver man to tear apart a curriculum, with its implied threat of power, status, promotion prospects and even, in some cases, to the livelihoods of the teachers involved. If possible, we all settle for a coat of varnish.

In discussing social change, R A Nisbet has emphasised the distinction between individual re-adjustment or deviance within a social system (whose effects, although possibly cumulative, are never sufficient to alter the structure or basic postulates of a society or institution) and the more enigmatic but fundamental change of type, structure, pattern or paradigm (Nisbet 1972). This distinction can be applied to the curriculum as between re-adjustment or deviance within the curriculum and change to the basic structure and postulates of the curriculum. Re-adjustment occurs when an individual teacher changes his syllabus or introduces a new teaching method which might possibly seem to some of his colleagues to be so radical as to be deviant. Change of this kind (even in the case of Christopher Searle) is acceptable as long as it can be contained, and does not threaten the basic structure and postulates of the curriculum as a whole, or the social structure of the school or college that is reflected in the curriculum. Schools Council projects on the teaching of a subject area, say, history or mathematics, are generally welcomed, because they can be contained within the curriculum, or, if necessary, quickly forgotten. Schools Council projects that integrate subject areas are less welcome (they cross Bernstein's boundaries) (Bernstein 1971), while the Council's suggestions for the reform of examinations have been greeted with prolonged and determined opposition, because such a reform would affect the basic structure of the curriculum and the power structure within the school. Most, if not all, curriculum change in the universities is also of the re-adjustment kind involving changes within rather than between departments. Joint degrees are generally only acceptable where they can be made up of bits of existing single honours courses. Interdisciplinary and unit courses are much rarer and are most developed in more recently established universities like Sussex and Essex where they were introduced at the university's foundation and

appropriate structures created to accommodate them.  Achieving
radical curriculum change in existing institutions is therefore very
difficult - so difficult that it usually only happens when precipitated by
a crisis.   By crisis, I don't mean a general, social or economic
crisis that demands a new educational response (this can be ignored)
but a crisis within the educational institution itself.  In the twentieth
century such crises have been brought about by the extension and democratisation of education.  When secondary education was extended with
the 1944 education act, a crisis in the existing grammar schools was
avoided by the creation of secondary modern schools.  The real crisis
came with the further democratisation of secondary education and the
creation of comprehensive schools, demanding a new curriculum and
new attitudes.  Even then some comprehensive schools have resisted
change, and have remained remarkably like grammar schools in their
structure and ethos.

Universities too welcomed the extension of higher education that the
Robbins Report promised, never realising the crises that this would
precipitate; more may not mean worse, but it certainly means different.
Tinkering with the university curriculum has done little to placate student unrest or to change the image of the universities;  so the government,
rightly or wrongly, has encouraged the expansion of polytechnics, which
it hopes will provide a new type of 'realistic' curriculum.

Teacher training has also been caught up in this democratisation
process, and this has resulted in a movement, albeit a somewhat
shambling movement, towards a unified, all-graduate profession.  The
major crisis in colleges of education came about with the extension of
the course from two to three years, followed by a dramatic increase in
the numbers of teachers trained accompanied by the introduction of the
B. Ed degree.   As with universities, the colleges accepted expansion,
but resisted any change to the structure of their curriculum.  Most
original Chippendale colleges consisted of ten to twenty staff, almost
all of whom had school experience. One or two, usually non-graduate
ex-primary school head teachers, became lecturers in education, and

the rest teachers of 'academic' subjects. But the main interest of all the staff was teacher training. The mathematics, geography or history lecturers, as well as the educational lecturers, would always have their eyes on the needs of the school. All the staff were involved in teaching practice. These small training colleges were therefore dedicated to concurrency. It was this which gave them their distinctive ethos. I am perhaps being a little romantic about this world we have lost There was, as we know, a darker and meaner side to the old teacher training colleges. However, the expansion of the sixties meant that the couple of education lecturers became a dozen or more, and, instead of an historian, geographer and mathematician, there were now subject departments each with its head and well-defined career structure. The organisation of colleges of education began to look very like that of red brick universities. It was at this point, too, that the universities began to exert an increased academic influence on the colleges. During the sixties university departments of education had also expanded, and in order to gain respectability they appointed, not experienced teachers, but educational psychologists, sociologists and philosophers and, in the larger departments, there sprang up sub-departments representing the so-called disciplines of education, frequently existing in isolation from methods departments and in isolation from each other. From these now rather self-consciously sophisticated departments there came a torrent of abuse about the 'undifferentiated mush' being served by mother hens to college of education students - mush prepared from corn packaged by the well-known firm of Hughes and Hughes. So the colleges also began to appoint sociologists, psychologists and philosophers, especially so after the introduction of the B.Ed degree. Meanwhile, the subject departments were also trying to prove that they were capable of degree work, and so they appointed young members of staff whose main interest and qualifications were in the subject itself and not in teaching it. In this process professional studies became a non-examinable extra and (as in the notorious case of the teaching of reading) no one was quite sure who was responsible for them. The fourth year of the B.Ed was concerned in all colleges with a study of the 'disciplines'

of education side by side with another 'academic' study. During this
year, in many colleges little reference was made to problems of teaching
and the students rarely if ever set foot inside a school    Concurrency had
become a confusion.   It was neither James nor the White Paper that killed
concurrency;  the colleges had strangled it before the James Committee
ever met.

I note, however, at this Conference (as always happens when colleges
of education lecturers get together) that there are those who are hellbent
on preserving concurrency. But what is there left to preserve? I don't
think concurrency is possible except in small monotechnic institutions
like Charlotte Mason, having designed a truly concurrent course, then
(to quote the Principal) 'proceeded to design and establish a completely
new staffing structure which required all staff to accept the ending of posts
then held and apply for new posts. It then planned an extensive and thorough
comprehensive staff development programme and restructured the constitution and composition of its Academic Board'. These are the essential prerequisites of a staffing structure that would suit the needs of a concurrent
course, and such a structure is just not possible in large diversified institutions. It would be better for colleges that are diversifying or joining
polytechnics to forget about concurrency and create structures that will
make consecutive courses work. This is a fatal moment to resist the
structural implications of the crisis that is besetting us.

Creating new structures is made difficult, not only because of split
sites and all the other practical problems affecting the individual institutions, but because we have so little, or no experience of creating end-on
teacher training courses which include a study of education integrated with
other academic studies during the pre-training period. Undergraduate
studies in education in universities are hardly developed, and, up to the
present, most education departments in polytechnics have in reality been
small colleges of education existing in isolation from the rest of the polytechnic. Polytechnic education departments have the same problems of
integration as colleges of education joining other institutions.

I would therefore like to spend the remainder of this article suggesting some organisational decisions which will have to be made if teacher training is to flourish in multipurpose institutions.

These decisions are, in my view, dependent on an interpretation of the nature of educational studies. By the end of the sixties a differentiated approach to educational studies had become accepted as normal. So much so that the practitioners of the various disciplines of education rarely spoke to each other, and certainly had little or nothing to do with methods lecturers or with teachers in schools. In 1973 Dr William Taylor was able to write about the 'role-specific knowledge' of educationalists, inspectors and teachers, so that the 'serving teacher who is widely read in the psychology and sociology of education, and who substitutes judgements from these spheres for the traditional recipie knowledge of the staffroom, may find himself regarded as an outsider, already half-way to becoming a college of education lecturer or local authority organiser' (Taylor 1973). In fact, the division between the teacher and the educational specialist is even greater than Dr Taylor suggests; it is not merely that the former uses common sense insights and the latter judgements based on scientific evidence, but that their problems and concerns are different. The educationalist at present has little advice to give the teacher or administrator to help them with their everyday decisions. And it is this, if our future courses are to be meaningful, that must change. Educational studies must be concerned at every level and stage with the analyses and guidance of educational practice. Educationalists must take up what Dr P S Wilson has called 'a practical stance'.

It should be noted here, however, that educational practice can include a vast range of activities - from teaching number in a primary school or organising a comprehensive school, to the Department of Education and Science deciding the allocation of resources to different sectors of the educational system. The distinction between educational studies at the training and the pre-training stage, is not that at one stage we are concerned with theory and at the other with practice, but that at the pre-training or generic stage we can include a wide range of problems and be concerned with them in a reflective way, whereas at the training or specific stage we must concentrate on those problems that confront a teacher or a specific age group or subject area in the classroom, and on the on-the-spot decisions that he or she has to make. The differences between the study of education at the pre-training and training stage are differences of focus and not differences in kind. Concurrence is dead, long live concurrence!

Such a point of view has at least two implications. First, education becomes an integrated study. Even Professor Peters, who led the attack against undifferentiated mush, has now recanted (Peters 1973). But, of course, we must try to ensure that the mush does not return. Meaningful interpretation is very difficult to achieve. We have all seen in schemes being submitted for validation, units in educational studies which, it is claimed, will be based on the insights of educational psychology, sociology, philosophy, but which give no indication of how these insights are to be obtained and integrated. My own view is that we should always begin with an educational problem and call on all those insights and methods of working that help to illuminate that particular problem. This may mean not only calling on psychologists, philosophers and sociologists but also on the insights and methods of historians, economists, and the subject specialists - mathematicians, geographers and so on. We must also call on the hard-won practical insights of the teacher, inspector and civil servant. With such an approach, deciding on the problem to be studied is, of course critical, as is the choosing of the techniques to be employed in gathering the data, and the skill used in getting the various specialists to share their insights and experience in interpreting the data. All this requires a course team chairman of exceptional skill and patience.

The second implication of this view of educational studies is that, if it is to be concerned with the analysis of practice, it must be based on practical work. This is as true of the pre-training as of the training stage. It is the emphasis of the practical work that will differ. At the pre-training stage the emphasis will be on analysis, at the training stage on putting the analysis into action At the pre-training stage the student will, to give an example, be concerned with studying the ways in which children acquire language and the ways they can be helped to do so - the student will be a participant observer. At the training stage he will be concerned with the problems which arise when he puts his knowledge into action as a learner teacher.

What then are the practical implications of all this? First, education departments must be organised in such a way that members are not isolated from each other. The larger the departments the greater the danger of this happening. The creation of inter-disciplinary problem-based courses should help avoid this danger.

Second, members of staff concerned with professional studies must, in my view, be members of the education department. I know that this raises difficult administrative and personal problems. Ideally, in a multi-purpose institution the geographer who is more interested in geography than the teaching of geography should become a member of the geography department. The geographer who remains in the education department should concentrate on the problems of teaching in general and on the teaching of geography in particular. You might protest that a continuing research interest in his subject specialism and contact with specialist colleagues will give the professional studies lecturer an added understanding of the problems of teaching his subject; the lecturer in geography method must understand geography as well as George. This is indeed so, but how many lecturers in professional studies have the time to carry out significant (or even insignificant) research in their subject if they are, at the same time, to keep abreast with such developments? It is research into teaching and curriculum development work that will illuminate the professional studies lecturer's own teaching - and win him the respect of his students and of teachers in school. Some new institutions of higher education have sought a compromise solution to this problem by creating a separate professional studies department. This seems to me to be the worst of all solutions, for such a department will inevitably become isolated from both the 'academic' departments of the college and from the education department (which will once again retreat into its ivory tower).

This will have a disastrous effect on teacher training and will create the situation that will lead to yet another committee of enquiry!

Third, the relationship between the college and the schools is now even more vital than it was in the past, and the organisational and financial structure of the college should facilitate this. Teachers and local education authority officials should be involved in planning and teaching courses, and certainly in planning and helping carry out the practical work that is part of those courses. So much of the practical theory that we all need in educational studies, concerned with the problems of teaching or school organisation, is just not available. We must create it. We can only do this in co-operation with the schools. We should not think of in-service training as a useful means of employing otherwise redundant staff, but as the central, essential activity that is going to make the creation of a body of meaningful, practical education theory possible. We should be establishing this co-operation with teachers now for it is such co-operation that is going to make the courses we create meaningful.

It will not have escaped you that I have skirted over most of these problems  In a sense there is little anyone can say until we have begun to put courses into practice, although it might have been more useful if I had spent my time in sharing with you the large failures and the small success my colleagues and I at Bangor have achieved in trying to integrate educational studies. It is obvious to me, as it was to Professor Alec Ross, that there is a need for a forum for just that type of discussion. I would support wholeheartedly the view that an organisation be established to enable those of us who are concerned with teacher education in multi-purpose institutions to exchange views about our practical day-to-day problems, to encourage development work on the periphery-centre, or periphery-periphery model suggested by Professor Becher. I hope very much that such a forum will soon come about.

REFERENCES

Bernstein, B (1971) Class, Codes and Control, London, RKP
Nisbet, R A (ed) (1972) Social Change, Oxford, Blackwell
Peters, R S (1973) Education as an Academic Discipline, British Journal of Educational Studies, volume XXI, number 2, June 1973, page 202
Taylor, W (1973) Research Perspectives in Education, London, RKP

# New Patterns

## M St J Raggett and M W Clarkson

One of the sadder facts to emerge from any consideration of teacher education at the present time is that what appeared to start as a movement to improve teacher education may have become little more than an administrative reshuffle of resources.   In this article we intend to return to what we believe is the central issue  -  that is how can the training institutions improve the quality of education and training of teachers?   We will do this by an analysis of the reasons why colleges have appeared to miss opportunities in the past;  by focussing on the problems of the products of the colleges in their first teaching appointments;  and by considering a model for teacher education which we suggest seizes some of the positive opportunities offered by the present cut-back in teacher education.

During the development of the educational system of the United Kingdom there have been many interesting decision points, for example during the early nineteen hundreds at the birth of state secondary education, or the development of the new universities in the fifties and sixties.   Another such period is now upon us with regard to the development of higher education.   We would argue that this present period of change is not just a matter of re-organisation of teacher education  -  it is about the total reshaping of post-secondary education.   This is an important claim but we believe that if this is so, we need to try to raise our sights from a consideration of the step by step changes that seem to be forced upon us to look for the wider horizons.   As David Hencke argues so persuasively, there seems to be a logic slowly emerging from a range of seemingly independent decisions about college futures which will affect the developing pattern of higher education. Indeed, we would argue that if one steps back even further one can see that there are elements of inevitability and inexorability about the events that are reminiscent of Greek tragedy.

If one extends the metaphor, once the Achaean's fleet had set sail, then for all the cries of Cassandra, unloved and unwelcome as always, the tragedy must take its course step by step. The battles fought and won on the plains are all irrelevant to the final battle. It is not the heroism of Achilles, the fury of Patroclus or the machinations of the intellectual strategist Odysseus (surely a candidate for Elizabeth House) that are important, but the restructuring of power in the Eastern Mediterranean and the spreading of opportunity by Aeneas as he sets out on his travels that finally result in the founding of Rome.

So it is with the colleges; their fate could perhaps be seen as a cutting of teacher training places to meet demographic changes and economic pressures. But this leads inevitably to the problem that one either has to cut out complete colleges or spread the cuts, when many may become too small to be viable. One does not need to be an organisational sociologist to see that the pressure for survival of the individual institutions will lead to the second being the more likely pattern and in turn leads to the need to find ways of merging the smaller institutions to create new larger and more viable ones. Perhaps this then requires one to change the balance of higher education. If so, the question arises, how have these demographic changes been articulated into the system?

Although insulated against most social pressures there has always been one pressure that has been implacable in bringing about change. This factor is the birth rate. Whilst colleges can ignore changes in the society in which they are situated, although at their peril they can only do so as long as their product matches the demands of the market place, on at least one dimension; quality or quantity, and the latter is probably by far the more important in practice. No concensus exists or is really likely to exist as to what is a good teacher, and so it is difficult to impose change using only this lever. But this is not true of the numbers argument.

Although the ideal class size may be in dispute there are limits and one does not need to be a very sophisticated mathematician to calculate that a rise in the birth rate of x% needs a parallel increase in the output of teachers. Unfortunately, in the colleges this process becomes even more striking due to what one might call the 'whip lash' effect. If the changes in the input to colleges could have been tied automatically and directly to the birth rate then the problems would have been difficult but not traumatic. Reductions or increases in the production of teachers tended to be more far reaching the longer changes were postponed. The decision of 1964 to go for all-out growth meant that colleges were jerked suddenly into an almost open door position with the intake of many staff who were snatched from the schools into rapidly growing institutions where quick promotion meant responsibility was soon thrust upon them. This was the generation who have created the present colleges and considering the enormous growth which took place so smoothly this was an undoubted achievement. The young ladies seminaries and cosy colleges of the late fifties became the 'modern management' establishments of the late sixties. The typical tutor of the fifties was the Mr (or Miss) Chips of teacher training; the new stereotype was the ex-head or head of department straight from school with perhaps more zeal than theory, more enthusiasm to do than wish to analyse. The introverted self-sufficient colleges changed to the self-confident boom-town extroverts.

But the birthrate has altered again and after the inevitable pause (for whatever reason) the realities of the market place have forced action and brought college closures, cuts and mergers. This leads logically to the position where we are now questioning the entire pattern of higher education. Is this stretching the argument too far? We would argue that if one includes other factors then it is not. The change in the economic climate is likely to mark the end of the period of unquestioned growth for the education budget in real terms and we are moving into a period when the distribution of these diminishing resources within the education system will become an even more critical question. This change makes a reassessment of our tri-partite system for degree work inevitable.

Universities, polytechnics and colleges and institutions of higher education represent an unnecessary multiplication of resources for a basically unitary market.  In any era of cost-efficiency a very careful delineation of objectives for the separate areas and co-ordination of effort is required. A second major factor is implicit in the former nil growth proposition. It is that if no further growth is possible then as new areas put forward claims for growth which other areas must be cut?  For this country this question is particularly acute as we do not yet have as high a proportion of of our eighteen- to twenty-one group in higher education as most European and North American educational systems  On the other hand there is a questioning of the simple notion that there is a need for growth at this level. We are now reaching a point where the marketing of graduates is becoming vital.  It is being argued in many circles that industry is already having to be persuaded to take the full output of graduates.  Serious consideration has been given to convincing smaller employers who would not normally employ graduates that they need to change their policies if they wish to find good candidates.  This inflation in qualifications is also resulting in the fact that graduation does not lead inevitably to high level, executive-trainee type appointments.  To put it bluntly, as the better A level candidates for posts in industry, banking, etc, are diverted into higher education, so employers need to raise their required qualifications to obtain the same quality of candidates.  All this suggests that consecutive higher education is not necessarily seen as a matter of real need at the moment  - a fact that is also evidenced by the fall-off in the number of applicants for higher education to below expected numbers. Indeed, the sixth formers may be following the curious pattern of preferring to join the dole queues to extending their education.  Perhaps one can understand that at a time of economic recession neither the DES, the employers nor the school leavers rate higher education as a top priority.  So one can see that changes in the pattern of teacher education may have been catalytic in sparking off a re-examination of the form of higher education, creating a period of internal crisis such as that referred to by Roger Webster in his article.  As David Hencke has written concerning the work of the James

Commiitte in relation to manpower planning ' . . . there is direct evidence of suppressed information presumably following decisions taken by ministers or possible even civil servants. Committee members were given access to the latest statistical trends which showed clearly that the DES was already aware that the expansion of teacher education would not continue indefinitely. Yet when the James Report was published, despite pressure from individual committee members, the public and the profession was denied access to this data.' (Hencke, 1975) Therefore the crisis had been foreseen and it would appear that those in Elizabeth House wished to conceal the main causal factor. The reason for this decision has never been made clear.

However this could become a time of opportunity, for it is only at such times of crisis that real change is possible, an interesting reflection on the whole area of innovation in the curriculum. As the IMTEC bibliographies show this has become the subject of a great deal of study but no simple formulas have emerged but it is not surprising for as both Roger Webster and Tony Becher imply one is touching on an area of great social complexity. Likely results of important curriculum developments at this level might be that the social structure of the organisations would be changed, including the power and status of the individuals involved. Indeed we find, to use Roger Webster's metaphor, we tend to apply another quick lick of varnish rather than attempt to rebuild fundamentally. This appears to be the situation even now in college re-organisation. Although, somewhat uneasily, a reconsideration of basic principles of teacher education is beginning. However, it is only occasionally one sees evidence of a commencement of a radical re-assessment of the effects of the release of fifty thousand places and their related resources on higher education. Although this is not the subject of this article there are only now beginning to appear interesting new projects and creative courses which perhaps show the opportunities being seized. Too often tedious involvement with the minutiae of change, motivated often by the need to ensure the minimum number of human casualties, has left the curriculum developers unable to take the broader view. Meditation is difficult when preparing a CNAA submission against the calendar.  Curriculum development takes time, dedication and skill, and the number of those capable, trained and involved is not large enough for creative thinking.

One of the ironies of the present situation that needs further exploration has been the lack of expertise in curriculum development in the colleges.   Whilst apparently being theoretical 'centres of excellence' - to refer back to Alec Ross's thesis  -  their lack of ability to sustain such a title has shown itself clearly in this field.   The college staff have often been only peripherally engaged in curriculum development work in schools and then never creatively as were those involved in this work in the Foundations or the universities.   Indeed, more of the project teams of the Schools Council or other bodies could have been located in colleges to promote a working understanding of the process amongst college staff. As David Jenkins has so neatly demonstrated, whilst the curriculum project visitor may have many problems when entering the social group of the school  -  college staff often have even more.   It would therefore have helped the college staff to enter closer relationships with active projects in schools.   So one can see that although the colleges were accustomed to change of a modifying type, real innovation, planning and implementation were to find them unprepared.   As in so many criticisms of the colleges, there was a grain of truth in the accusation that what the college staff taught was book knowledge, not experience-based knowledge.   Now this lack has become a problem to the colleges as they find themselves moving into a period when this particular set of skills, deriving from curriculum development experience is needed for developing new courses and entering into a dialogue with the CNAA.   A small group of tutors has grown up in many colleges who have developed an expertise in this area to meet the need but only as a result of dedicated work on the part of these tutors.   As this group has often not been the same as those organisationally in positions of power in the hierarchy, it has led to the growth of conflicting power base in the system  -  a power derived from the 'expert' group's control of the specialist knowledge required in the rapidly changing situation.   This group has been identified by sociologists in other areas, for example, Gouldner's reference to the 'expert executive' in his study of a factory as a social system (Gouldner 1957). He suggests that the 'expert' relates to an outside group with whom mysterious skills are held in common. In this case one can see the 'new men' are acting as 'gatekeepers' to the new futures for the colleges and their colleagues and are likely to be both loved and feared as a result. Their titles may be 'course co-ordinators' or 'curriculum development tutors'; or no title at all. However, by reason of two factors the power of these individuals to shape and decide the future of their institutions has grown rapidly. First, they have been able or willing to devote the time to attending conferences, reading papers and meeting those outside their own organisations who have the power to influence its future. Secondly, they have created a sea of complex paper within the colleges, in which their colleagues, including the senior members of the colleges have found it difficult to appreciate a pattern, much less the subtleties. Thus the 'new men' have developed a professional circuit of specialists including not only the 'curriculum developers' in the colleges but also, we would suggest, such external figures as the members of the Foundations involved in projects such as STEP, members of the Regional Advisory Councils, DES Inspectors in this area, and a few correspondents and publishers. Two comparable groups elsewhere spring obviously to mind. As many political diarists have confirmed, the civil servant can influence the decision-making of his minister by the way the case is presented and choices limited, and similarly the local government official preparing papers for his committee. In a like manner the 'expert' tutor by his awareness of the multiplicity of external constraints can limit the choice of an academic board so that only the desired decision can be reached. When questioned reference to external legitimating bodies will ensure success. It is difficult to argue against reference to CNAA guidelines if one is neither familiar with their comments nor the 'case law' associated with them.

It is therefore our contention that the pressures on the colleges have upset their ability to cope with tactical and strategic decision making.

It has been argued that the senior administration's role is to cope with environmental and internal uncertainties but in this instance they have not done so. Why has this largely occurred? We would argue that the ability of the decision making structure to cope with unpredictable problems has been thrown by the radical nature of the environmental change. It is not just a change in the rules - the whole game has been changed. Principals and academic boards are the supposed guardians of the strategic decision making but this is only possible where they have both the positional power and also power deriving from knowledge. It is not sufficient to have the constitutional power within the structure to make the decisions as both the principal and the academic board undoubtedly have - it is also necessary to be able to frame the decisions so that they match the 'critical path' of events and the constraints of the outside world. To do this one needs the necessary knowledge. It is this separation which has hamstrung most colleges, we would argue, in taking the broader and more creative view of their futures, for the guardians of the broader perspective are separated from the skills of the curriculum developers - and both perhaps have become separated from the body of the staff. This process of estrangement can be seen firstly to be increased by the jargon differentiating the 'new man' from the other two groups providing the curriculum group with a perceived professional language or register of their own. Secondly, it is also increased by the insecurity of the tutors with regard to their ability to hold on to their positions. Redundancy fears can put pressure on internal social relationships. If positional power is subject to negotiation in its exercise between the holder and those with whom he interacts, uncertainty as to the individual's tenure of the position is likely to affect his power within the negotiation. The power held externally to manipulate uncertainty, in this case held mainly by the DES and the LEAs, is therefore a further factor. This particular power has been exercised widely by the DES and it has only been pioneering work of the kind described by David Hencke that has in any way affected its creation and continuation of uncertainty. To use a different form of analysis one can see this as a classic example of the conflict between the professionals (the tutors) and the administrators (the hierarchy in the colleges) or at another level between the college staffs and the LEAs and the DES. Some individuals or institutions have shown themselves more able to cope with this uncertainty but overall it is clear that the internal interacting phenomena could be seen to inhibit the likely creation of a coherent and long term policy.

Thus the continuing uncertainty of the changing relationships within the colleges have meant that responses to the unparalleled opportunity for creative thinking in higher education have, with a few noticeable exceptions, tended to be mundane and unimaginative   This field is notably missing bold suggestions for the use of fifty thousand diversified places which will now be released. In the case of these courses, in part the blame may be placed at the door of Circular 6/74. Insisting that new advanced courses can be squeezed from existing staff and resources may be good resource management but it is hardly likely to lead to the creation of inspired and imaginative courses. Link to this the external legitimating bodies' obsession with student availability and graduate employment prospects, it is no wonder colleges have played safe and reproduced their existing teacher education main subject courses as new degrees and avoided the harder, more perilous development of new and untried areas. But our concern here with diversified courses is only where they affect teacher education courses in the new institutions and there the suggestions seem to be mainly concerned with juggling with basically unchanging units of training. No rethinking of a dramatic kind to match the opportunity seems to be present. For example, why colleges as physical entities at all? Perhaps this may seem too radical a question. Again, what evidence is there that any initial training is of value? This is clearly asking fundamental questions of a kind we are not competent to answer here. But who is? One can question the unthinking belief, we would argue, that the more initial training the better.   As the James Committee stressed, and many agree, highest priority should now be given to the expansion of opportunities for the continued education and training of existing teachers. This appears to derive from a widely held belief that they  -  separately from their initial training  -  develop  practical skills.     When these have been acquired the teachers can as 'journeymen' return from time to time for a further injection of theory which will revitalise them for many years.

On examination this view of teacher education has its underlying model clearly exposed. The model suggests initial training is merely a conditioning process which enables students to undertake the apprenticeship in schools after it is over. It presupposes the education of teachers should only be about 'how' and not 'how? what? when? and why?'. The colleges have a broader view of teacher education as education and not training. The teachers tend to see it only as training. It is indicative of this that large numbers of teachers still talk about 'teacher training', 'training colleges', and 'in-service training'. The colleges see this initial foundation period as one when the fundamental issues of education can be raised and the student encouraged to develop himself fully as an individual. There is not a single aim, therefore, but two; training and education going hand in hand. One thing is clear, however, and it is that colleges need to re-examine the basic models for teacher education held by themselves and teachers in the schools, if only to lay some of the criticisms held so widely of initial training. If both sides realised that they have totally different conceptions of the aims for teacher education and these were made explicit perhaps a more informed debate could take place. It is probably unlikely, however, that teachers in the schools and tutors in the colleges will ever agree for they have basically different responsibilities. The teachers' first concern is their pupils and they thus have an instrumental view of teacher education as an efficient training preliminary to release into the schools with a licence to practice. The tutors, on the other hand, have the added dimension of seeing the students as their 'pupils' for whom they have educational responsibilities of an individual kind. These two perspectives will therefore often tend to conflict.

John Wilson writes that ' . . . we are in a mess; a mess which it is our first duty to sort out for practical purposes, and which has to be sorted out before we can do anything sensible'. (Wilson, 1975) This rather emotional assessment is one in a series of assessments of teacher education that offer little to solve the basic difficulties of which many within teacher education are fully aware. How does one take an eighteen year old sixth form pupil and in three years produce a mature, sound teacher? How can one give experience of 'going solo' in one of the lonelier jobs without leaving the young adult to crash to disaster without help? How can one develop the teaching skills without a sophisticated understanding of the social and sociological constraints upon their effectiveness? Indeed, how can one teach a teacher what, and how, to teach and more important, when and why to teach it? Those within colleges of education may have perceived the problems, have tried to solve them but often found the teachers the first to question their methods and block their experiments. This attitude often appears to derive from teachers' suspicions of initial training per se. A college tutor once described how his label as a practitioner underwent a radical change to that of a mere theoretician in the eyes of his colleagues in the course of a summer vacation. He had simply moved from being a head of a primary school to being an education tutor in a local college of education. This distancing of those responsible for initial training is a curious phenomenon which magnifies the problems of the college staff in a frustrating manner.

However, this dichotomy exists and although a severe constraint on creative experimentation in the colleges and university departments it will not be solved until the twin problems of rational questioning of the efficiency of the courses and the teachers' irrational antipathy to tutors are resolved. What needs to be done at the present is first to rethink the basic education of teachers ruthlessly and then to ensure that the positive creation of new courses is in accordance with a model for courses the teaching profession will accept. In order to do this it is necessary to look more closely at the basic problems that teachers meet in practice and experience at their entry to the profession, and then look at the implications. A necessary return to fundamentals is something that Skilbeck, for example, would suggest is basic to effective curriculum development. The situational analysis prior to commencing defining aims and objectives has often been a one-sided affair considering much more the constraints of college resources than the discovered needs of the new teachers. Dale, Bolam, Raggett, etc, have offered evidence in this area but it seems to have been ignored. What then happens to new teachers?

When the ex-students enter teaching, they have to accept certain changes imposed by the 'arena' in which the interaction is going to take place. These changes in context, in this case, can be summarised as being threefold. First, the beginner teacher will have a change imposed on him as to his degree of responsibility for the work in the school. He may find that he is responsible, almost totally - and from the very beginning - for a whole class in a primary school. At no time as a student will he have been given a personal responsibility of this order, and this increase may be both drastic and even daunting at first.

Secondly, the beginner teacher has to look a different set of 'significant others' in the sense Mead uses this phrase. This applies to both 'peer group' (in this case those with whom the student/teacher is working) and also to those with power to define his situation for him. In college, as in his previous experience, his 'peers' who acted as a reference group were normally a homogeneous age-group; in whom he might readily see himself reflected. Now he has to accept that his 'peer group' is no longer age-related and his 'peers' or 'colleagues' are a social group dependent rather on a common occupation. Colleagues may be fussy, conservative teachers who fear innovation as they await retirement, dynamic executive-model career teachers, or uncommitted housewives who 'lodge their selves' in their out-of-school roles more than in teaching at all. Amongst such a diversity of colleagues the young teacher may see no one who can be said to reflect himself as he has so far perceived himself.

Thirdly, another major change in context for the teacher is that he is now responsible for his own learning; that is, he must define for himself what is relevant knowledge in a way that he may never have had to do before. When at school himself, and even in college, he will have had others attempting to define areas of knowledge for him, and even if this is rejected, it may be seen as a reaction to an offered pattern. Now, on the other hand, even though he may hear some 'staffroom' advice, it is up to him by himself to define those parts of educational theory, practice and knowledge of the particular children that he considers relevant to his new status.

From research we have recently been engaged in at Brighton, we have developed an analysis based on three stages, which serve as a useful tool for considering the critical initial period:

a) Initiation - the presentation of the new world to the teacher;
b) 'Internalisation' - the period during which the personal redefinition of the ex-student as teacher takes place;
c) Evolution - the movement out of change into a relatively stable definition which will only slowly change over the years.

The first is the stage when the young teacher is presented with the material with which to construct his interpretation of the school. In some schools this may involve him reading through school prospectuses, 'notes for probationary teachers', listening to an introduction to the school by the head, attending an initial staff meeting, being briefed by his head of department, attending a pre-term conference for probationers, etc. However, as well as this formal set of organised interactions, there will also be the informal, from which he may draw a different set of perspectives. The discussions with fellow teachers, overheard discussions in the staffroom, visual material on the noticeboards, the symbolic nature of so much that he sees and hears will 'present' a reality to the young beginner which he orders into his own personal construction. He makes sense of what he perceives in his own particular way - and this is obviously affected by what he brings to this situation. Recently, with the growing awareness of the critical importance of this period for teachers, there has been an increase in the formalised initiation procedures. However, one result of formalisation of initiation can be, if it brings together enough probationers, the creation of awareness and possibilities for communication between them. This can help to support the young teachers in creating their own particular perspective on the environment in which they find themselves. The arena will be seen in the wider context of the profession, enabling the growth of different understandings perhaps than those which the initiators of the meetings may have wished to create.

'Internalisation' is the second aspect of the change process. During this period the personal redefinition of the ex-student as a teacher is taking place and this is where the process of socialisation is seen to 'bite'. However, as Howard Becker in an article on this area (Becker, 1970) points out, 'the self . . . is constantly changing, and, in this sense, the label "adult socialisation" is a misnomer, suggesting as it does the process occurs only occasionally and then only in special places'.

In fact it is clear that socialisation into the new status of 'teacher' occurs at varying speeds - initially slowly during training perhaps, but definitely at greater speed during the adaptation period of the first term and slackening later. The beginner teacher in his or her responses to our research often revealed evidence of still thinking as a student even at the beginning of the first term, of failure to realise the need for self-structuring of much of teaching. For example, the cry for a syllabus, for more guidance: 'After seven weeks' teaching in a London junior school, A stream, 9/10 year olds - I still have no timetable from the headmistress'. Others quote similar needs and are almost shocked to find they are no longer in a 'six weeks and out' situation but need to plan for the longer term.

Indeed, the entire process of 'becoming a teacher' involves severe risks for participants It is not simply a passive role where one is imprinted with the correct reflexes but it is a social learning situation. This is perhaps part of the contribution of teachers' criticisms of teacher education courses in that they are more keenly aware of this aspect. The individual finds himself having to make responses and act out in public the 'role' of teacher with only a minimal 'internalisation' of this having taken place. The entire construct may break down - and break down in public. The situation in itself requires a degree of commitment that is difficult to simulate. Sanders makes this point clearly in a different context. 'A bomb defuser, for example, must display a calm, steady hand while he detaches wires and fuses from explosive packages. His actions function in two importantly different ways. On the one hand, shaky movements may set off the bomb and, on the other hand, such nervousness reveals a weakness of character. In either case the trembling defuser blows his performance, pointing to an instrumental as well as an expressive stake in acting calmly'. (Sanders, 1973)

Similarly, the young teacher in the classroom may 'blow' his performance at a critical juncture and shatter the carefully structured presentation of himself as a competent performer. And it is not only in the class room that the new teacher has a new 'self' to present; in his interaction with colleagues and parents he must crucially present sophistication of a degree that will force these 'significant others' to accept his presentation for the purpose of the interaction. All this he must do whilst still having only partially 'internalised' this novel perspective of himself as 'teacher'. Not only this but the others with whom he has to interact, teachers, parents, pupils, are not always prepared to help him to adjust. Thus the new teacher has a high risk element built into his situation. A nice example of this can be seen in this description of one of our respondents in her problems with parents during her first term: 'I left college still feeling very much a student rather than a teacher, and this undoubtedly manifested itself at the beginning of term and gave some parents the chance to come in and try and make me work for them, rather than for what I considered to be for the good of their children.

This emphasises the lack of definition by the teacher of herself as teacher and the way that the definition of herself as student is only slowly fading. However, it is not long before the teacher begins to make a provisional 'internalisation' of the role. Finally, however, usually by the end of the first term, the beginner teacher has reached a point where he has accepted a self image that matches the image others have of him in the social context he now finds himself.

Thus one turns to the period in this critical year which leads on into the future career of the teacher. The pace of change slows and the formation of a stable definition of himself as teacher will be related to the perception of the context in a way that is personally acceptable and yet is also congruent to the broader group perspectives of the relevant others.  This stage will probably most often be reached by the beginning of the second term when the teacher will be beginning to look beyond the school itself to the wider context of the profession.  He will then have reached some kind of definition of what he considers relevant knowledge to his role and will wish to fill perceived gaps some of which will relate to his specific context but others will be of a more general nature.  For example: 'The only aspect of teaching that has been a problem are the parents.  The college at no time gives advice on how to deal with problem parents (and in many cases they are more of a problem than the children)'.  Another example concerns relations with the pupils: 'Never realised before how important it is to have knowledge of homes, etc. Knowing how to react to particularly forthcoming children is difficult, what to say to a child who says "My dad 'it me 'cos I hit my dad, 'cos he was hitting my mum with a belt" - child aged five;  and "My mum didn't do anything.  Why does my dad hit my mum?".'

These situations are probably difficult not only for beginner teachers and are perhaps indicative of a movement towards acceptance of a wider group perspective of teachers in the specific school.  For what is important is the way the individual school's conception of what is involved in being a teacher becomes assimilated by the young probationer.

We would therefore argue that in considering the whole process of the induction into the teacher's role, the third stage identified by our research in Brighton has important implications for teacher education. First, the process of 'initiation' implies that the young teacher arrives at the institution in which he will begin his career with a sense of being very much external to it.  It can therefore be argued that there needs to be much more inter-penetration of the schools and colleges so that there is a breakdown of the present harsh dichotomy.  The boundaries of teacher education have been dissolved for some time now.  The old model of a college as almost a country house party for young ladies, frozen in time, has crumbled. As an institution so uncritically linked to school teaching the colleges have always continued to take their model from the schools who fed them. During recent years it is obvious that they have changed their role model from convents and the direct grant school, and now, to the comprehensive school. No longer are they secure in their belief that they are taking the best pupils. In the past by reflecting the grammar or direct grant schools they offered an elitist education and prepared their students for a life in schools separate from the majority of their pupils. As recently as 1960 at least one college was insisting on long gloves and dresses for dinner and finger bowls on the high table. This might have been an acceptable introduction to teaching in some public schools but not one for urban secondary moderns. Schools and colleges had become separate, drifted apart by the currents of society and the colleges were circulating in an eddy by the bank whilst the schools were being swept remorselessly onwards.

Today therefore there are both the needs and opportunities to increase the amount of interpenetration between schools and colleges for a variety of reasons. First it is clear that pupils in the schools, reflecting changes in the broader society are presenting different problems to teachers. Secondly, and it is really another facet of this same broader change, teachers have different attitudes to pupils. They are torn much more between their idealistic conceptions of their role, and the herculean task of trying to implement innovation in the face of rapidly growing constraints. The simple role of the teacher as the liberator of the oppressed society or even as the dispenser of social justice is now, thanks to the growing corpus of research, seen to be a way set with thorns. Now the more percipient are aware that even the estimate they make of the pupil's ability may affect his performance and life chances Yet action of some sort is felt by many teachers, especially the younger, to be not only necessary but the only way to survive in the escalator of a changing society. In education there has developed a paradoxical belief that those who stand still fall behind. If this is so where are the colleges? It would appear that now is the time for another lurch (lurch can be defined as an illco-ordinated movement towards the schools if the colleges are not to become more and more out of touch. William Percival put forward the metaphor of the battlefield to describe the situation in colleges with the individuals ducking and weaving as they ran from shellhole to shellhole. Although perhaps a picturesque metaphor it may illustrate the difficulty there has been for the colleges to remain centrally interested in the educational problems of schools whilst fighting for their own survival. In devising the ploy and counter-ploy of the battle some of the broader educational issues may have been missed. Indeed there has been a tendency to meet all the recent developments with the question 'Will this mean more students for us?' This has been unfortunate, but very natural. However, what is needed now is to release the impetus for curriculum development towards the schools.

How can more effective links be achieved? First and most obviously there is a need to separate clearly the teacher education element in the colleges from the diversified courses and offer a much greater partnership to teachers in the planning, implementing, assessment and evaluation processes. Secondly, there can be greater involvement by students in schools. There will be one benefit at least of the fifty per cent cut in student numbers, as the cuts work their way through the colleges, the numbers of students needing school places will drop. This will therefore ease the pressure on schools and should ensure that they would be able to accommodate greater student involvement without disruption. This is an opportunity for a partnership between the schools and colleges to plan the extra schooltime imaginatively. What is needed is to direct the creative ingenuity of the college curriculum developers to offering student involvement in schemes that make a positive contribution to local schools.

The second major stage identified in the Brighton research was 'Internalisation': that is the period during which the ex-student accepts that he is in fact a teacher. This is a very important change as it is from being the taught to becoming the teacher; from being the acceptor of authority to becoming the authority figure; from being the immature member of society to one holding an adult position from within it. The implications for teacher education are important for this is a change for which the colleges need to prepare the student   Since the move to greater self-responsibility by the students which culminated in the traumatic disputes of the late sixties, the pace has slowed and the rearguard has successfully fought the movement to a standstill.  Indeed, in the most important area, the courses themselves, there have been very few real attempts at staff/student participation in the colleges.  The teaching is still too often much nearer the sixth form pattern, and not even the best sixth forms.  What appears necessary is a much more 'adult' approach to the students in the colleges and by this is meant two things.  First that the organisation of the learning should be much more at the level one would offer experienced teachers.  Secondly, there should be a definite programme during the first year to change the incoming students' perception of the colleges into that of an institution which is part of the broader continuing education and not only the initial training of teachers   This could be aided by the involvement of larger numbers of teachers in college courses not only as in-service students themselves but as contributors.

This leads naturally to the third major stage identified at Brighton - the evolution of the student into the teacherly concerns of the experienced teacher.   Here again one can see how the colleges could offer probationers in-service opportunities, in conjunction with the teachers' centres and schools, to act as a lead-in to natural participation in a pattern of continual retraining and re-education during their whole future careers.  It is clear that during the first year young teachers often find certain specific areas in which they need further direct practical knowledge.   Examples of this might be related to aspects of the teaching of reading and particular Schools Council Projects being used in their schools.

Thus one can finally see that a pattern emerges.

In order to improve the quality of initial training one wishes to see the students in the schools for longer periods.  At the same time, and arising out of a conjunction of needs one wishes to see more teachers in colleges - not just as visitors but involved in courses. This can be represented by the following model of the process:

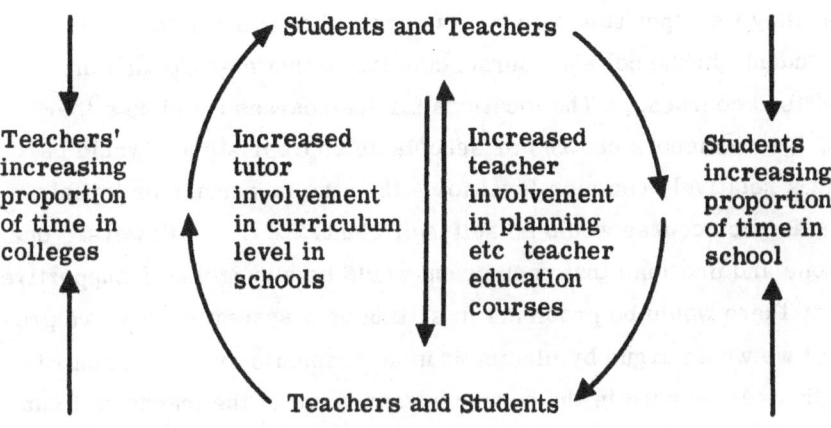

But let us be practical and consider how this may be done. First one must ensure that teachers get a return for co-operation with the colleges. They will wish to see a good reason for them to take part in the courses created by the colleges whether these are located in the schools or the colleges themselves. It is likely that those courses in the schools will be of immediate professional relevance but the courses run in the colleges will probably be of a more general level and of not such imminent interest. How can we ensure teacher participation?

One way we would suggest that would help to integrate in-service work into the new structures would be to offer credits for modules of college courses which the teacher has completed satisfactorily. If the teacher completes a number of courses these credits could be put together to make a qualification such as an 'In-service Certificate' or 'In-service Diploma.' For example, a teacher might attend a second year course in linguistics, a third year course in special education and in-service courses on management of learning and organisation of resources in schools, and receive an 'In-service Certificate'. The courses might be a minimum number of hours in length, for example, thirty hours, and with only forty per cent tutor contact time. The teachers might find that they were perhaps only two or three among fifteen to twenty initial students in the college courses and the opposite proportion in school-based courses. The locations for the courses could be either college, local teachers centres or schools as appropriate and would be aimed at a relatively common level for either the in-service or initial students as each course would be self-sufficient. However, one would hope and presume that each group would be strongly self-supportive. Obviously there would be problems in setting up a system such as we propose, but we would argue by placing it in an academic system of qualifications that can be used in the career advancement of the teachers it can offer a relevance and a value to in-service education and initial training which at present is missing.

So what we would propose is needed now is a positive effort to encourage a movement towards each other of the schools and the teacher education faculties of the new institutions. This needs to be a criterion for the validators of the new courses, a goal for the designers and a rule of thumb for the implementors. It should be an aim consciously pursued by the NUT and the LEAs. However it ought to be recognised that this can be sincerely desired by all parties but will not necessarily succeed unless there is a genuine acceptance of each other's problems between schools and colleges and rather more mutual respect between teachers and tutors. As the Induction and In-service Training Sub-Committee of the Advisory Committee on the Supply and Training of Teachers suggested in the discussion document on in-service education and training: 'There is clearly much to be gained in relating initial with in-service education; not only will teaching resources be more widely used but more important, a more formal relationship than has existed hitherto should provide tutors in colleges and departments of education with new opportunities of contact with schools and serving teachers and in turn will establish a framework in which teachers can contribute more regularly and effectively to initial education courses.  A common use of resources should in itself facilitate a better understanding and a more fruitful professional exchange between those who teach primarily in schools and those in colleges and departments'.

Perhaps our final conclusion should be that despite the opportunities that have been missed in the past for reasons now becoming clearer, by looking first at the ethos of teacher education and then at the problems of the probationer, we can begin to construct a more positive model which may help us in the future.  For too long we have considered it through the eyes of a latter-day Cassandra seeing only gloom and despondancy as the old order changes, whereas we should be seeing it as a time when the inflexible structures have become more fluid and the opportunities are there if we can recognise them.  To return to where Norman Mackenzie started we can indeed sympathise with the man on the Titanic.  We expected change but we have been presented with a peripeteia.  But it is often by seizing the opportunities presented by such changes of fortune that one can build anew this time, not merely apply a new coat of varnish.

## REFERENCES

Becker, H (1970) Sociological work (British Edition) Harmondsworth, Allen Lane, The Penguin Press

Gouldner, A W (1957) Cosmopolitan and locals: toward an analysis of latent social roles in Administrative Science Quarterly, December 1957

Hencke, D (1975) Re-organisation of the colleges of education in England and Wales, Higher Education Review, Autumn 1975

Sanders, W B (1973) Pinball occasions in BIRENBAUM, A and SAGARIN, E (Eds) People and places, London, Thomas Nelson & Son

Wilson, J (1975) Educational theory and the preparation of teachers, Slough, NFER

# Contributors

NORMAN MACKENZIE   Professor of Education and Director of the School of Education, University of Sussex

DAVID HENCKE   Correspondent of Times Higher Education Supplement

JAMES PORTER   Principal of Bulmershe College of Higher Education

ALEC ROSS   Professor of Education, University of Lancaster

EDWIN KERR   Director, Council for National Academic Awards

ANTHONY BECHER   Professor of Education, University of Sussex

KENNETH GARDNER   Senior Tutor, Brighton College of Education

WILLIAM PERCIVAL   Principal of Charlotte Mason College of Education

NORMAN EVANS   Principal, Bishop Lonsdale College

BERNARD FISHER   Principal, City of Leicester College

ROGER WEBSTER   Professor of Education, University College of North Wales, Bangor

MICHAEL RAGGETT   Senior Lecturer in Education, Brighton College of Education

MALCOLM CLARKSON   Academic Registrar, Brighton College of Education